BELIEVE & LIVE

BELIEVE & LIVE

A 31-Day Devotional on the Gospel of John

BY J. ROGER DAVIS

Published by Iron Hill Press

Published by:

Believe and Live: A 31-Day Devotional on the Gospel of John

Published by Iron Hill Press and printed in
the United States of America.

ironhillpress.com

Library of Congress Cataloging-in-Publication Data is on file
with the Library of Congress, Washington, DC.

ISBN: 978-1-970539-04-2

Cover design by Faceout Studio.

Table of Contents

Introduction

If you have ever read or heard stories about Jesus in the Bible, they have likely come from one of the four Gospels. The Gospels are the first four books of the New Testament and tell the story of Jesus: His life, ministry, miracles, death, and resurrection. At its core, the word "gospel" translates from Greek as "good news." The first three Gospels, Matthew, Mark, and Luke, are more similar in structure and in their treatment of the narrative of the life and death of Jesus, and are referred to as the Synoptic Gospels. When set side by side, the similarities in their content become very apparent. The first three Gospels give particular attention to Jesus as King, Servant, and Son of Man. But then there's the fourth Gospel, the Gospel according to John. John's recordings of Jesus' time on Earth offer a different perspective of Jesus and His life, with a specific focus on Jesus as the Son of God. It is of utmost importance to note that none of the four Gospel writers is telling a different story. They are sharing the *same* story from a different *perspective*.

The Gospel of John is widely accepted as written by John, the youngest of the disciples. He and his brother, James, lived with and traveled with Jesus for about three years of Jesus' public ministry before His death. The writer of the book is traditionally referred to as John the Evangelist or John the Apostle. However, he referred to himself as "the Disciple whom Jesus loved," or a variation of that, six times in the Gospel of John. I am sure that if you or I had referred to ourselves like that growing up around our siblings, it would have stirred things up. John may have been trying to be humble, or, as he later wrote and reflected on his time with Jesus, he simply knew the reality that the Lord deeply loved him. Regardless of why he referred to himself that way, there is little doubt that John, along with his brother James and Peter, formed a close "inner circle" for Jesus. This proximity allowed him to witness countless miracles and moments with the promised Messiah.

Can you remember anything about elementary school? I like to think of John like the kid in school who had that big box of 64 Crayons with the built-in sharpener. While the rest of us are working with the basic box of eight Crayons full of mostly primary and secondary colors, John is giving us a picture using every color available to him. The author does not merely record the acts of Jesus and present a linear storyline from His birth in Bethlehem to His death at Calvary. He wants to make sure that the mystery of Jesus the Christ is clearly and fully revealed to the reader (we will talk more about that in just a bit).

Each week of this devotional, we will clearly see the central theme of John's book: the divinity of Jesus, God becoming flesh, and dwelling among us. The one true God, trading in a robe of glory for a robe of flesh. An amazing concept to wrap our heads around, not just on Sunday mornings or as a random thought here or there, but for every moment of our lives. Additionally, we will see together the themes of eternal life, light overcoming the darkness, becoming a witness for Christ, and the call for all of us to be people of love. Whether you're a person who has grown up in church, a new Christian, or just curious about Jesus, the Gospel of John is for you. It's good news for all of us. I hope that as we study it together, the good news will work deep in us and through us.

Each day, we will take some time to journey through the 21 chapters of John. We will read some verses from the book and reflect on how they reveal who Jesus is and how He relates to us. At the end of each day's devotional, there will be some questions to help you think through the message of the verses and some thoughts or prompts to help you communicate with God. Prayer, which is simply a two-way spiritual relationship in which we give our attention to God to both listen to and talk with Him, is an amazing gift He gave us. This devotional will help you see how the truths found in John apply to your life today, and I pray that, once you know the truth, it will set you free.

About the Cover

Many roots of the early church are found in modern-day Türkiye, including the church at Laodicea, mentioned by the Apostle John in Revelation 3 and the Apostle Paul in Colossians 4. In 2020, archaeologists discovered the ruins of a Laodicean house church, now known as the "Peristyle House with Church," or "House A." Its size suggests it belonged to a wealthy family in the first century AD, and it is believed that several house churches existed in the city.

I visited Laodicea with pastor friends a few years after this discovery. I took the photograph on this book's cover from the first room of that house, looking back toward the entrance, where a pronounced lintel is framed by the rising morning sun.

The city was a prosperous commercial center but had no natural water source; it relied on aqueducts to bring in water that started cold in the mountains, but by the time it reached the city through clay pipes, it was lukewarm. It was a fitting illustration of rebuke (Rev. 3:14-21), with the term "Laodicean" still used today to describe someone who is lukewarm or indifferent in their faith.

John's Purpose

Day 1

John 20:30-31

As we read the Gospel of John, it is important to ask, "Why did John write his Gospel?" The other three Gospels, the Synoptic Gospels, were believed to have been written before John's account. With the first likely being Mark, then Matthew, Luke, and then John coming fourth. In school, you often find it is easier to get the correct answer when you look in the back of the book. So, while you typically start with the first chapter when reading a book, to understand why John wrote his Gospel account, we must go to the end. Let's get started.

Begin by reading John 20:30-31.

Have you ever pulled up to a stoplight and the person in front of you has a custom license plate that says something like "HYUDEWN" or "DOIKNOU?" Or maybe they want you to know they are a fan of a certain team and you see, "HKYNUT," "YNKEFAN," or "COWBOYS." Maybe they just want you to know their name, so you see "IAMMATT" or "MR BILL." You may know these are called vanity plates, and for a few extra dollars at your DMV, you can decide what you want the world to know in seven characters (within a few guidelines).

One of my good friends, a teacher, has a vanity plate on his car that reads "JN20 31." My friend, just like the disciple John, wants to make sure everyone knows that "*Jesus is the Christ, the Son of God, and that by believing you may have life in His name.*" That is why the book of John is written, that you would believe, that I would believe, and that all the world would have a chance to believe. Living in His name is a personal relationship with the only true God, revealed in Jesus Christ.

John shares with us a dynamic and distinct picture of Jesus that, while consistent with the other Gospel writers, more deeply reveals Jesus as the Christ, fully God and fully man. If John were writing a marketing blurb or web copy and had to provide a purpose statement, it would be simply, "Jesus is the Messiah, the Son of God." This is not just a conclusion at the end of the writing, but the entire foundation and focus that John establishes for all who read his Gospel account. Throughout the book, he reveals to us that Jesus is the long-awaited Messiah, the promised one who takes away the sins of the world. He does this by sharing and showing various messianic "signs" or miracles of Jesus, as well as the words of Jesus, pointing to the importance of believing in Him and the gift that comes from that belief.

Belief, however, can be only yours. It does not matter what your spouse, your children, your pastor, your co-workers, or even your friends to the left or right believe. In the end, it matters what you believe. Your faith must be yours.

If Jesus is who the Bible says He is and who He claimed to be, the Son of the living God, then the only logical response is to trust Him as your Savior and Lord. To have life in His name. I pray that, as you read this book, you and your faith will grow in a new and dynamic way.

Reflection

1. When you hear the gospel is called "Good News," what does that mean to you personally?

2. Who do you believe Jesus is? Where are you currently finding life?

3. What do you hope to get out of this journey through John over the next four weeks?

Prayer

If you have placed your faith in Christ, thank Jesus for leaving Heaven and coming to Earth to live the life He lived so that you could be with Him forever in eternity. If you are not sure whether you have faith, ask God to give you an open mind and heart for whatever He has for you over the coming weeks. Pray and ask God whatever you want, knowing He is available to listen and wants to talk with you.

Day 2 The Word Became Flesh

John 1:1-5

Begin by reading John 1:1-5.

Each year, during the Christmas season, it is likely full of traditions like favorite holiday movies, Christmas sweaters, shopping, favorite foods, family get-togethers, gift exchanges, singing Christmas carols, and the story of Jesus being born in a borrowed manger in the town of Bethlehem. The nativity scene has been part of the Christmas tradition since Saint Francis of Assisi created one in 1223 to convey a clear picture of the meaning of Christmas. Since then, nativity scenes have become a part of many Christian homes and churches in various shapes and sizes. The Gospels of Matthew and Luke mention Bethlehem and Jesus' birth to the virgin Mary in that Jewish village, just five miles south of Jerusalem. The Gospel of Mark does not include any birth narrative. And then there is John.

John does not take the reader to the little town of Bethlehem on a silent, starry night. He takes us all the way to the real beginning, showing a direct link between the nature of God and the nature of the Word, Jesus the Christ. Re-read John 1:1-2. John will highlight at great length that Jesus is the Word incarnate (in the flesh or in human form), but in these first words, he shows Jesus as eternal and already existing with God, tied to the opening words of Genesis 1:1.

You may have read them before, but take a minute to go back and read the first verse of the Bible. Do you see the connection that John makes with the language, *"In the Beginning"*? John highlights the interpersonal connection of the Word (Jesus) with God. This is also a foundational building block of the doctrine of the Trinity. That is, the one true God exists in three equally divine Persons, the Father, the Son, and the Holy Spirit. The Trinity can be difficult to wrap our minds around, regardless of our age or experience. However, the Bible is clear that all three Persons are each one-hundred-percent God rather than each being a third of God.

Look once more at Genesis and check out verse 1:26. Who is God the Father talking to? While the text does not specifically give the identity of the "us" here, He is talking to Himself...well, kind of. He is talking to the Ones there with Him in the beginning. That would be a Trinitarian Council of God the Father, Jesus (the Son), and the Holy Spirit. Here in the first chapter of the Bible, we see the first evidence of this foundational truth. We will have some more time to explore this together later in our study.

Back in John 1:3, we see what God made: all things. That means God created everything in the entire universe. It was all created by a creative God who merely spoke, and it came to be, while He worked in unison with the Son and Spirit. It's also important to note that when God creates things, they are good, as Genesis 1:31 states: *"And God saw everything that He had made and behold, it was very good."* God does not make mistakes. He does not need an eraser, a mulligan, or a do-over. Everything He makes is not just good; it is very good. That is also a reminder to you that you were created by a God who makes good things. I don't know what you think about yourself, but it is always good to be reminded that you are no mistake. You are created and loved by God.

John closes the introduction of his Gospel by also connecting to Genesis through the concepts of life, light, and darkness. Jesus is the "light" coming into the world, introducing the reader to the truth that life can be found in Him. This is a reality that Jesus will also share in His own words later in John. Light, by nature, reveals darkness. You can see that as well back in Genesis. God continues to call His creation good, but there is no mention of darkness being good. God creates a clear separation between light and darkness, and only one is called good.

In the Bible, we see separation created between light and darkness, not just in the natural sense but in the spiritual sense. Darkness does not drive out the light; it only comes when the light leaves. When light shines in the darkness, however, things begin to be revealed.

Reflection

1. Why is it important to believe that Jesus was in the beginning rather than just showing up on the scene for the first time in Bethlehem?

2. How do you view yourself in relation to God's role as the Creator who makes good things?

3. When it comes to your personal theology, your organized beliefs about God, what is foundational for you?

Prayer

Take some time to praise God as the amazing Creator that He is. Thank Him for sending the very best to us in Jesus, the incarnate Word, God in the flesh. Ask God to help you work out what you believe over the next few weeks about Him, Jesus, the Holy Spirit, and living as an ambassador of light rather than in darkness.

Day 3 A Witness to the Messiah

John 1:6-34

Begin by reading John 1:6-28.

Have you ever heard of the Biltmore Estate in Asheville, North Carolina? It was built starting in 1889 and officially opened for friends and family on Christmas Eve, 1895, by its owner, George Washington Vanderbilt II. The massive Châteauesque-style mansion is a whopping 178,926 sq. ft. with 250 rooms, and it's listed as the largest privately owned home in the United States. Years ago, I was there visiting, and as I took it all in, I came across a very small plaque with a quote that the owner was fond of saying: *"There are two ways of spreading light: to be the candle or the mirror that reflects it."* I went later that night and wrote it down in my journal as I reflected on those two roles, the light and the mirror.

John 1:6 introduces us to a wild man known as John the Baptist or the Baptizer. This John, you need to know, is not the same John who wrote the Gospel we are reading together. This John was a cousin of Jesus and reacted in his mother Elizabeth's womb when she was in the presence of Mary, who was also with child (Jesus) at the time (Luke 1:41-44). I like to think of John the Baptist not just as a messenger preparing the way for the Lord, but also as a mirror reflecting the beauty of the light.

John bears witness to the light that has come into a darkened world. Pay particular attention to verse 8 in John Chapter 1, and then to verses 19-21. It is important to know who we are and who we are not. John the Baptist understood his role. As we read through today's verses, we see the repetition that began at the beginning of John's Gospel: that John the Baptist was to be the witness of the one to come.

In Prague, Czech Republic, a large bronze statue of John the Baptist was built in 1857 on the north side of the river at Charles Bridge. The artist, Josef Max, could have depicted John the Baptist in numerous poses, but he simply portrayed him holding a cross in his left arm and pointing with his right index finger. That pose effectively highlights John the Baptist's role. He simply pointed to Jesus as the long-awaited Messiah.

"And the Word became flesh and dwelt among us." An important question to ask is, "Why did Jesus come into the world?" It was more than just giving us something to celebrate each year at Christmas; so much more. John shows us that Jesus' own people did not receive Him, but to all who do receive Him, to each of us who believes in Him, He gives us the right to become a child of God. That is a statement we must let marinate; it must soak in. The God who created everything and controls all things has given you and me the chance to be called His child. Don't miss that gift.

Between the Old and New Testaments, there is a time of waiting of roughly 400 years. It is called the "intertestamental period," and the waiting was for the promised one, the Messiah who was to come. This is why the priests and Levites came to John the Baptist and inquired about who he was, because he had been stirring up the system and sparking a lot of conversation among the established leaders. If you look in your Bible between the books of Malachi and Matthew, you will likely see a white page or a transition page. Just remember that this page is very, very important. It represents those four hundred years of waiting.

Continue reading John 1:29-34.

When John finally sees Jesus with his own eyes, how does he immediately respond? He identifies who Jesus is, "the Lamb of God," and that He "takes away the sin of the world!" Jesus is the total message, everything that God the Father wants to communicate to His creation. For generations, a growing number of people had continued to widely disregard the message of what must have seemed like an invisible God and instead lived in their sin, selfishness, and rebellion. But everything changed when the long wait was over, and Jesus put on a robe of humanity. The struggle about to unfold, however, is that many people in that time of waiting hoped for a king who would conquer earthly oppressors.

In summary, the Word (Bible) points to the Word (Jesus), John the Baptist points to Jesus, and Jesus points to God. Jesus, while becoming man, never ceases to be fully God. He made His dwelling with us. God with humanity. The truths presented by John can clear the theological fog many find themselves living in. And the truth is that, while Jesus might not have been what was expected, He is no doubt exactly what was and is needed.

Reflection

1. If you thought of your life as a mirror, what would it be reflecting?

2. If you thought of your life as a witness to something or someone, who would your life be pointing to?

3. John knew who he was and who he wasn't. Why is it so important for followers of Jesus today to know their identity in Him before they try to "shine" for Him?

Prayer

Think about your view of Jesus. What does His coming to Earth mean to you personally? When you point to Him, what is on your mind and in your heart? Do you know Him in a personal way, or is it just what you have heard from others? If you know and realize that you are a child of God, that is an amazing thing. That simply comes by confessing with your mouth and believing in your heart. (Romans 10:9.) If that is not something you have done before, I encourage you to read through the section on page 125 in the back of this book.

If you are already a Christ-follower, I encourage you to offer a prayer of thanksgiving to God for your salvation, and then a prayer of availability. Let God know that you are ready and available to do His work. Ask God to use you to prepare the way and make straight paths for the Lord in connections and conversations with your friends and family. The Lord wants to use you to point to His Son, Jesus. Are you willing to be like John the Baptist and embrace the role of the messenger, pointing to the message?

Day 4

Two Words That Will Change Your Life

John 1:35-51

Begin by reading John 1:35-42.

Last time, we were introduced to John the Baptist. In today's reading, we see Jesus beginning to assemble His core team, which is referred to as the calling of the disciples. None of us needs to be a technology historian to conclude that, during Biblical times, there was no social media like we have today. But there was still a reality of having followers. One crazy thing to think about is the fact that John the Baptist had a growing number of followers. When Jesus began His public ministry, John encouraged them to unfollow him and begin following Jesus.

In this passage, Andrew and another unnamed disciple of John encounter Jesus. Jesus asks them an important question. This question is not just important for these two, but also vital for each of us. "What are you seeking?" Jesus asks. Most of us, as well as anyone we encounter, are seeking something. That could be acceptance, love, popularity, riches, happiness, freedom, peace, fulfillment, confidence, etc. The list is almost endless. As humans with these desires, we often look high and low to satisfy them, yet we often find disappointment and emptiness. To find something that brings the fulfillment we desire, it is important to seek it in the right place.

These two disciples quickly realized there was something different about the Teacher in their presence. Might it be that this Jesus in front of them could be the long-awaited Messiah? Andrew runs to share with his brother, Simon, and proclaims, "We have found the Messiah." The term Messiah, which means "Christ" or "Savior," conveys the idea of "anointed" by God. The Old Testament predicted and prophesied of the coming "anointed one" from the lineage of David that would save the people of God. In the New Testament, the "Messiah" was the long-promised one we have already begun learning more about in our reading together. It is important to know that Christ is not Jesus' last name; it was and is His position. We also see here Jesus giving Simon a new name, Peter, meaning "rock," as he will become a trusted companion and champion of Jesus.

Continue reading John 1:43-51.

When Jesus meets Philip, He gives the simple call, "Follow Me." These two simple words will change Philip's life, the rest of the disciples' lives, and yours as well. It is a life-changing call that Jesus still gives. As Jesus gathers His disciples, we see an interesting pattern that continues throughout Scripture and even into today. It is a cause-and-effect of "come and see," then "go and tell." A friend of mine once said to me, "Found people become people finders."

Nazareth was not mentioned in the Old Testament and was a town of little importance. When Jesus was growing up there, it likely had about 2,000 residents. Because of its lack of distinction, it was more likely to be included in a joke than to be recognized as the place that the Messiah would spend His adolescence. It catches Nathanial by surprise, and Jesus repays that by blowing his mind when they meet. At the first meeting, it is evident that Jesus already knows him, and then He describes where he was with an "I saw you," which again shows Jesus' supernatural knowledge. Interactions like this helped validate that Jesus was the anointed one. As the disciples were amazed, it must have brought a small smile to Jesus' face. He tells them, "You will see greater things," as He knew what was coming. Have you ever thought that Jesus wants to show you greater things?

In conclusion:

Jesus knows your name.

Jesus knows your past.

Jesus knows your future.

Jesus gives you a new name.

Jesus is ready to show you greater things.

Reflection

1. Does your relationship with Jesus touch every aspect of your life?

2. What are you seeking daily? Matthew 6:33 reminds us, "*But seek first the kingdom of God and His righteousness, and all these things will be added to you.*" How is that showing up in your life?

3. Peter gets a lot of publicity. He is bold and often a bit loud. But what if Andrew never brings Peter to Jesus? It is easy to focus on the people we know in the world, like Peter, but don't miss your opportunity to be an Andrew for someone.

4. Have the words "follow me" become a reality for you and your life?

Prayer

Think about what your daily life looks like and where Jesus shows up in it. Share a word of thanks to the Lord that He knows your name and your future. If you have been seeking things other than the Lord, confess that to Him and ask for forgiveness. Ask the Lord to help you seek Him daily.

Day 5

The First Miracle of the Messiah

John 2:1-25

Begin by reading John 2:1-25.

The four Gospels together record 37 total miracles performed by Jesus. Mark's Gospel records the most, with 24, and in the book of John, we see John highlight seven miraculous signs that occur outside natural law. Miracles are recorded to validate the authority of the one performing them; throughout the Gospels, they highlight Jesus' power and purpose.

In John 21:25, John says, "Now there are also many other things that Jesus did. Were every one of them to be written, I suppose that the world itself could not contain the books that would be written." Based on this statement, what we see and know is just a glimpse of all that Jesus did. Here are the seven miracles found in the book of John:

- Turning the water into wine (2:1–11)
- Healing of the royal official's son (4:46–54)
- Healing a paralytic at the pool of Bethesda (5:1–15)
- Feeding the 5,000 (6:5–14)
- Walking on water (6:16–24)
- Healing the man blind from birth (9:1–7)
- Lazarus raised from the dead (11:1–45)

In today's devotion, we are focusing on what is considered the first miracle Jesus performed at a wedding in Cana.

In John 2, we see Jesus, His mother, and His recently called disciples being invited to a wedding at Cana in Galilee. Cana was in what is now northern Israel, about 5 miles from where Jesus grew up in Nazareth. While we don't know the identities of the bride and groom, they were likely relatives or friends of Jesus' family, given their proximity to His hometown and the invitation extended to His mother, His friends, and Himself.

It's important to know that in the Jewish culture of this day, weddings would often span multiple days, usually five to seven, and typically, the entire village would gather for the wedding celebration. What's even more important to this story is that wine was at the core of the wedding experience. As part of Jewish tradition, the couple would drink from a shared cup of wine, symbolizing the life they will share and create together. This is something you may also see at a wedding today. Wine often represented joy in Jewish culture. A common thought was that without wine, there is no joy.

So, here in John's account of the wedding, Jesus' mother realizes they have run out of wine, and something needs to be done before it becomes an embarrassing situation. She comes to Jesus and tells Him that they have no wine. What Jesus says next, I would not encourage us to respond to our mothers in the same way. He simply says, "Woman, what does this have to do with me? My hour has not yet come." We need to note here that Jesus was always about the Father's timing. He was fully submitting to the Father's will. It is also good for us to be reminded that God is always on time.

If anyone knew who Jesus really was, it had to be Mary, the mother of Jesus. After all, she was the teenage girl who an angel visited and told her that God was going to place His Son into her womb, and she would give birth and raise the promised Messiah. A scary proposition, but one that had to increase her belief and knowledge of who Jesus really was. In John 2, she does not respond to Jesus' question, but simply speaks these wise words to the servants, "Do whatever He tells you" (verse 5). In these next moments, we see Jesus giving clear instructions, and He delivers the first public sign of his divinity. The Bible says it "manifested His glory," which simply means it revealed it. At His mom's request, Jesus transforms approximately 120 gallons of ordinary water into wine, and the quality is so good that the master of the feast praises it! Remember, to Israel, a world without wine symbolized a world lacking joy. You and I need to know that there is no true joy without God's blessing. Jesus has joy by the barrel, and He freely gives it away.

There is a lot for us to digest in this story before we move on today. We see Jesus attending a wedding of someone with whom He had some type of relationship. This is a great reminder of the personal and communal connections that Jesus has with His people. This act of kindness Jesus performs shows that He cares about the everyday problems and issues His people face. Jesus can provide for our needs. He provides for basic needs throughout Scripture because He longs to provide for His people's deeper spiritual needs. This first miracle also clearly grew the faith of His new disciples, and I hope it is also a step in growing our faith as we read along.

The bigger your view of God gets, the more you want to trust Him. The smaller your view of God is, the more you want to control things. John puts a spotlight on a very BIG God and his divinity.

Reflection

1. When you consider the miracles of Jesus, what thoughts come to your mind?

2. How did these miracles validate Jesus' authority and divinity?

3. When you think about God's timing, do you trust that He is always on time, or do you doubt Him?

4. Do you think Jesus' first miracle, at a wedding, is significant? Why or why not?

5. Do you have joy in your life? Would you consider that joy abundant?

Prayer

Think about Jesus, and if your view of Him is full of awe and wonder. Is that a reality for you? Or is Jesus more of a historical figure who did cool things? As you pray today, tell Jesus what you honestly think of Him. Let that lead your prayers in this moment, and then listen to what He has to say in response.

Day 6 Not in My Father's House

John 2:13-25

Begin by reading John 2:13-17.

Up until this time, Jesus had spent most of his life in the northern region of Galilee, with His hometown of Nazareth being 163 kilometers (91 miles) north of Jerusalem, which is in the southern part of what in ancient Israel was called Judea and where the Temple was located. The two regions are separated by another called Samaria, which we will read more about later. Some time has passed since Jesus' first miracle at the wedding in Cana, but that experience has likely not helped Him stay under the radar as He begins what will now be known as his public ministry.

During Passover week, Jerusalem would be like a vacation hotspot, filled with out-of-towners. You will notice the text says, "Jesus went up to Jerusalem." This might seem odd because Jesus had been in the north and was traveling south toward the city. Typically, one would say, "I am going down to the beach" if traveling south, or "I am going up to Michigan" if traveling from the south. However, Jerusalem, as a city, sits on a mountain range surrounded by lower valleys. When one traveled there, they would have to travel up to get to the city gates.

When Jesus gets to the city, He goes to the Temple and its large courtyards. Jesus was very familiar with the city and the Temple. One of the most significant visits to the Temple was when he was 12 years old, accompanied by his parents, who brought him to town for the Feast of the Passover (recorded in Luke 2:39-52). During that experience, His parents left town, unaware they were returning home without Him. If you remember the story, when they returned searching for Him, they found Him still in the Temple, "sitting among teachers, listening to them and asking them questions." Those elders that he was around had their minds blown at the knowledge and understanding of this 12-year-old boy from Nazareth.

One important thing to note (which comes up again in our reading today): when Jesus' parents found Him, as any good parent would, they were worried and told Him they had been looking everywhere for Him. Jesus responded, "Why were you looking for me? Did you not know that I must be in my Father's house?"

What greeted Jesus on this trip to the Temple was not pleasing to Him. The massive crowd of pilgrims was buying animals at a premium for sacrifice, since those who had not brought their own were not allowed to sacrifice. Lines of people filled the Court of the Gentiles, exchanging money with high commissions to pay the Temple tax. Jesus immediately began driving the moneylenders out.

This response was not Jesus just flying off the handle and going nuts like a western bar fight. He was strategic and controlled, taking the time, "making a whip of cords," and driving them out of the Temple, turning over the money-changing business. What was Jesus' problem? It was not just about the crowds gathered in the Temple, but also about the corruption and greed on display. He knew what the Temple was, and again, here, He reminds all who would hear Him, "Do not make my Father's house a house of trade."

Continue reading John 2:18-25.

Jesus knew that some would believe in Him if they saw signs and wonders, but that belief would not transform them as much as it would wow them. He would often share with the crowds, the religious leaders, and even His core group of followers statements that did not make sense to them. This is because they were always thinking on an earthly, "known and seen" level, while Jesus was speaking on an entirely different level: a heavenly, unknown and unseen realm. We see this at play here as Jesus tells them He will rebuild the Temple in three days; they quickly respond with a, "Come on, man; it took 46 years to build this thing."

While it is easy to think these guys just don't get it, remember that you and I get to view things through the lens of current knowledge. We know about the cross and Jesus taking on death and rising on the third day. The disciples of Jesus did not fully understand it in the moment, but later, when what was unknown became known, they remembered this declaration.

As Jesus and His teaching became better known, He would retreat from the crowds, often because of timing or trust. Jesus was always about God's plan and God's timing. And with divine knowledge, He knew the thoughts and hearts of people. In Greek, it would mean that Jesus did not believe in them. He could see the hidden motives of man and would not give Himself to their temporary faith. Furthermore, He was also not dependent on their approval. It is also a warning to us that desiring the approval of man rather than God's approval can be a massive barrier to belief.

Reflection

1. When you think about how much Jesus valued the Temple and it being His Father's house? And what can you take away from this and apply to your life?

2. What do you have to see from Jesus to truly believe He is who He said he was?

3. Do you trust God's plan and God's timing in your life?

4. Do you seek approval from the people around you more than from God who created you?

Prayer

Ask God to reveal to you new truths about who He is and your view of Him. Consider what areas of your life you need to pursue holiness in. What are things that you have not valued as much as you think you should? Ask God this week to work in those areas of your life. Close your time in prayer today, telling God what you want to say to Him as you look to Him rather than those around you.

Day 7 The Original Nic at Night

John 3:1-21

Begin by reading John 3:1-14.

John is such a rich book, and there are so many things that you can study and learn about in John's Gospel account beyond where we focus our attention each day. In these next few devotions, we're going to focus more on the signs and teachings of Jesus as His ministry and following grow. We will begin to see more of His interactions not only with the disciples who have been called to follow Him and learn, but also with others. Pay close attention to how Jesus treats and talks to people.

Today, we are introduced to a Pharisee named Nicodemus. I like to think of him and this interaction with Jesus as the original "Nic at Nite" rather than the block of TV programming from Nickelodeon that debuted in 1985. The Pharisees were a Jewish sect that could be kind of a mix of a priest and a lawyer. They paid close attention to outward appearance and lived by a set of rules. They believed they were not only right in their teachings but also above others because of their authority in the community. This set them on a collision course with the presence and teachings of Jesus.

The Pharisees listened to Jesus and did not like what they heard, as they felt it did not align with their teachings and interpretations of Scripture. As Jesus' popularity among the people increased, they lost followers, and unlike John the Baptist, they were not happy about it. This made Jesus a hated enemy of their leaders.

However, some Pharisees were intrigued by what Jesus was saying. Some even began to question their own understanding, and others even embraced the teachings of Jesus and recognized Him as the Messiah. That was a difficult affirmation, and to do it publicly would risk losing their identity. That includes our friend Nicodemus, whom we meet in today's reading, who comes to Jesus under the cover of night.

Nicodemus was called a "leader among the Jews," which meant he was not at the bottom of the organizational chart but was likely a higher-up. He was even a member of the Sanhedrin, which is the powerful political council of the high priest. An example we might be more familiar with would be the United States Supreme Court. Needless to say, Nicodemus was a big deal.

In his first recorded interaction with Jesus, we see that he was impressed and recognized that something about Jesus was different, even from God, as he says. But was he fully convinced that Jesus was the Messiah? Jesus begins talking about childbirth to this Jewish leader. His illustration is confusing because any of us who know basic biology understand that a person cannot enter their mother's womb and be born again. One thing we need to acknowledge is that when Jesus is speaking with people, they are thinking about earthly realities, but Jesus is speaking about a heavenly reality. This is something we too need to grasp as we read Scripture.

In this encounter, Jesus uses the term that you may have heard in or around church, "born again." This is a reference to not being born physically; we know that has happened once for every person, but being born anew spiritually. Jesus is talking about a spiritual birth, and if that has not been a reality for someone, they will not enter the Kingdom of God, and they will not be made right with God through Jesus. We see this in two important references. First, in verses 13 and 14, Jesus references the Son of Man. We likely understand "Son of God" as referring to Jesus' deity, but "Son of Man" also refers to His humanity. Remember that Jesus was fully God and fully man. Then, in verse 14, "so must Son of Man be lifted up." Can you think of what that might be referencing? Jesus says something similar again in John 12:32, "And I, when I am lifted up from the earth, will draw all people to Myself."

Continue reading John 3:16-21.

John 3:16 may be a verse you have heard before, or at least wondered why somebody is holding a posterboard with John 3:16 written on it at a sporting event. It is widely accepted that this verse is the most popular Bible verse in the world. In this verse, we see the gospel clearly laid out. Martin Luther, the great church reformer, said that John 3:16 is "The heart of the Bible, the gospel in miniature." The great evangelist Billy Graham spent 58 years of his ministry focused on this verse and its provision for all people. In the book of Romans, Paul calls salvation a free gift (Romans 5:15-17), but here in John, we see that it comes at a great cost: it costs God His only Son, Jesus.

Because of the popularity of John 3:16, we often miss the richness of John 3:17 and beyond. So many people in the world believe that God (and therefore His followers) condemns them, but in fact, He sent Jesus so that all could be "born again" and saved. Jesus does not condemn people in this life, but they can be restored and redeemed by the blood of the Lamb.

Often, people think that the gospel is judgmental and cruel. Some will even ask in their disbelief, "How could a loving God condemn people?" But the truth we see in these verses is a loving God sending His Son, not to condemn, but to restore all His children to Him. Jesus is raised up, taking on the cross of Calvary, so that everyone can realize the Kingdom of God. New life from God comes through the power of the Savior's sacrifice. But many, like the Pharisees, think their way is better.

Reflection

1. The term "Son of Man" is referenced over 80 times in the Gospels. Why does it matter that Jesus was fully God and fully man?

2. How do you balance the concept of salvation being a free gift, but also costing Jesus His life?

3. Nicodemus came to Jesus at night, possibly out of fear of being seen. What are some ways fear, comfort, or reputation can keep us from fully coming to Jesus in the light today?

4. Jesus told Nicodemus that he had to be "born again." What might that look like in your daily life (emotionally, relationally, or spiritually) to live as someone made new in Christ?

Prayer

There are many different types of prayers we can offer to God. Still, a simple way to structure your prayers is to use a model that has been utilized by the church for countless years and comes down to these four focuses: **A**doration, **C**onfession, **T**hanksgiving, and **S**upplication (ACTS). Think through those, and pray through each one below.

Adoration: Tell Jesus you love Him. Share with Him your thoughts about who He is. Acknowledge His greatness.

Confession: Acknowledge your weakness. Have a moment of honesty with God and share with Him what you need to. John reminds us in 1 John 1:9, *"If we confess our sins, He is faithful and just to forgive us our sins and to cleanse us from all unrighteousness."*

Thanksgiving: Moving from who God is, we now thank Him for what He's done. Thank God for sending Jesus into the world to save you. Offer any other prayers of thanksgiving that are on your heart.

Supplication: This is where many start, bringing requests to God. God wants to hear from us as His beloved children, but it is a good thought to begin with the others before our list of needs. Pray for your own needs or for those of others on your mind.

Less of Me and More of Him

Day 8

John 3:22-30

Begin by reading John 3:22-30.

John shares more about Jesus' work in Judea, including His baptism ministry. We all find ourselves living in a culture of competition and comparison. This mindset causes us to look to others as competitors, competing for followers, resources, recognition, the job we have always wanted, someone else's affection, or a way to get ahead of those around us. In addition to causing unhealthy stress, it can lead us to set unrealistic expectations for ourselves. The disease of comparison is not an official medical diagnosis, but it is a reality that affects many.

The rise of social media has accelerated this unhealthy habit in our society. We scroll and see others' vacations, new cars, fun lives, and families that seem to have zero problems. Others' highlight reels woo us. We think that so many have it better than we do. Many even count followers like currency of self-worth, a validation of their voice. This is a trap the adversary loves to set regarding our identity.

John the Baptist, whom we encounter in our reading today, had been baptizing before Jesus' public ministry began and had continued that sacred practice. He had a deep understanding of who he was and who Jesus, the long-awaited Christ, was. We can almost feel the tone of some of John's disciples as they began questioning why they were all just sitting around while their team was losing momentum, as well as that of many supporters, toward the new guy on the scene. Rather than being frustrated or envious that he was losing these followers and focusing on his ministry to Jesus, John showed great humility and great love in his unwavering commitment to the supremacy of Christ. He reminds his team, "A person cannot receive even one thing unless it is given to him from heaven."

John's words are an important reminder to each of us. John the Baptist knew his identity and his role was to prepare the way and proclaim that the Messiah had come. As a key part of that declaration, he understood and joyfully announced that Jesus must increase, and he must decrease. This was a key transition in ministry; it was time for Jesus to be center stage.

When I was younger, I had a coach who would often say, "I need more than 100% of you." If you have been around sports in any capacity, you, too, have likely heard similar. But in reality, there is only a 100% that makes up who we are in body, heart, mind, and soul. The decision each of us has to make is whether we are going to hold on to it all, acting, in essence, as if we are the king of our life, or are we willing to decrease, giving ourselves over to Jesus as the *King* of our life. This is, for sure, an identity shift, one that is polarizing to a culture of competition. But this is what it means to be surrendered to Jesus' Lordship over your life. When we do, we discover that less of us is more in God's hands.

Reflection

1. If you compared how you view those around you with your own self-view, how do you think you would score on a scale of 1-100?

2. John the Baptist understood who the giver of all good things is. Do you know and acknowledge where good things in your life come from?

3. When you think of your identity, how do you not only understand who you are but also live in that assurance daily?

4. What are areas of your life that you must decrease so Jesus can increase?

Prayer

Ask God to forgive you for any time you have fallen into a spirit of comparison. Give Him thanks for all that He has provided for you in your life. You may find benefit by saying areas of provision by name. Ask Him to reveal areas today in your life where you need to step back so Jesus can step in. Today, look for a day of discovery of places you need to decrease. Less of you and more of Jesus.

Day 9 Good News for All of Us

John 4:1-30, 39-42

Begin by reading John 4:1-30.

Have you ever gone out of your way to avoid someone? Maybe it's walking a different way at work to avoid that person's area, or driving a different route to make sure you don't end up in a place you don't want to be. Today, we are looking at an amazing interaction that Jesus has with a Samaritan woman at a well. For a Jew to travel from Judea, in southern Israel, to Galilee in the north, they would usually go out of their way, walking around Samaria to avoid interacting with the people who lived there. Jews considered Samaritans to live by a lower standard, as they practiced slightly different religious beliefs. They believed that God lived on Mount Gerizim, as we see highlighted in today's passage, but the Jews believed that God was to be worshiped at Mount Zion in Jerusalem. Most Jews felt it was best for them not to interact with Samaritans in any way. But Jesus ignored the expectations about who He was to avoid.

We see the humanity and divinity of Jesus in His interaction with this woman. Jesus was thirsty because He had been traveling, and it was around noon (that is, the sixth hour), likely the warmest part of the day. It is important to realize that this woman was going to the well alone in the heat of the day, the least desirable time to draw water. All of the other women had likely come and gone, but she was evidently an outcast with her own people. Jesus engages her in a conversation about water, and it becomes another one of those moments where she is thinking earthly, and Jesus is talking heavenly.

In verses 16-19, we see Jesus' divinity and omniscience as He asks her to get her husband. Omniscience simply means "all-knowing." He knew her reality before He asked her to "call her husband, and come here." This prompts her to quickly realize that there is something different about the man talking to her. Jesus continues by contrasting the different holy places of worship for Jews and Samaritans, but a new reality is coming. It is so important that we do not miss verses 25 and 26 because some say that Jesus never claimed to be the Messiah. You can't read and believe this story and agree with that. He clearly identifies Himself as the Messiah.

We see a similar pattern to what we saw when Jesus first called the disciples. After seeing and interacting with Jesus, she left her water jug and went and told the others in her village. Come and see. As we discovered previously, found people become people finders.

Continue reading John 4:39-42.

Don't miss that God used a Samaritan outcast woman. Neither of these would have been the social norms. Because of her words and testimony, many people in her village believed. She did not have to be a vocational minister or have the right training to begin telling people about Jesus. She just shared that Jesus "told me all that I ever did" and loved her anyway. That is the truth about Jesus, regardless of your past, your position, or your popularity. Jesus sees you, loves you, and wants to be in a relationship with you. That is good news for all of us. The invitation: Come and See. The response: Go and Tell

Reflection

1. In this story, we see Jesus interacting with the "least of these." When you think about the least of these in your weekly interactions, who would those people be?

2. What are your current interactions with those people, and is there anything that needs to change?

3. What does this story tell us about who salvation is for?

4. Does God's omniscience scare you or give you comfort?

Prayer

Ask God to show you people in your average week who may be outcasts and need to be shown love and for the gospel to be shared with them. Ask the Lord to give you the courage to be willing to show that needed love and to share the gospel. Thank God for His presence and provision in your life, and for knowing everything about you and loving you anyway. Share with God anything that is on your heart.

Time for the Harvest

Day 10

John 4:31-54

Begin by reading John 4:31-38.

Anyone who has been camping for an extended period of time understands the need to go into town to get food and supplies. The disciples were likely a bit cautious as they navigated the unknowns of Samaria, including entering a village for food. Once they returned from town, they encouraged Jesus to eat, but He again threw them for a loop when He told them He had food they didn't know about. Again, if you have ever been camping, it is quite a discovery to find out someone has a secret food stash in their tent or bag.

The disciples were confident that Jesus did not have food before they went to town, so they wondered if someone had brought Jesus food. That might be a reasonable possibility in Galilee or Judea, but it is highly unlikely in the more hostile Samaria. But what the disciples had not yet picked up on is that Jesus is not talking about the sustenance of physical food, which is a necessity for life, but about a spiritual feeding that nourishes the soul (we will explore this more in John 6). Jesus knew well "that man does not live by bread alone, but man lives by every word that comes from the mouth of the Lord" (Deuteronomy 8:3).

Again, Jesus exemplifies full submission to the Father. Jesus was not against food or eating; we see this, of course, in numerous other examples, including His first miracle at the wedding in Cana. What Jesus is saying here to His disciples, and us, is that not only does provision come from the Father, but people are waiting to hear the life-sustaining good news of the gospel. Jesus is addressing a hunger that is deeper than one for physical food. And just as He encourages His disciples on that hillside to see themselves as Kingdom workers, He calls all of His followers to embrace this mission.

Continue reading John 4:39-42.

Before we move on with our reading today, I think it is important to highlight that in this passage, the Lord once again shows His care for all, regardless of social standing, skin color, or financial realities. He stunningly did this in this passage, as He worked through the most unlikely source: a Samaritan who was also a woman. The gospel was once again spread by someone that society would call an outcast. The Samaritan woman was excited by her interaction with Jesus, and we see the power of sharing the good news with others.

Finish reading John 4:43-54.

As I travel around the country, I enjoy looking at the various state license plates with unique designs and state sayings. The plates and slogans reflect a wide range of features, from historical events and cultural uniqueness to natural elements found in each respective state. I imagine you know at least your home state, but could you also identify others with their corresponding states? Would you know which state "The First State" belonged to (Delaware)? Or to "The Last Frontier" (Alaska)? Would you recognize the "precious metal" states, such as "The Silver State" (Nevada) or "The Golden State" (California)? Surely you could identify "The Lone Star State" (Texas) or one of my favorites, "The Volunteer State" (Tennessee). These slogans often connect personally to the people who call each state home.

One state slogan I have always found interesting is Missouri's. The "Show-Me State" slogan is said to date back to 1899, when U.S. Representative Willard Duncan Vandiver expressed skepticism in a speech about certain claims. It is reported that he said, "I am from Missouri; you have got to show me." This statement is said to have existed before he memorialized it in his speech, but it stuck and became a nickname for those from this Midwestern state.

While ancient Israel did not have a slogan like the various United States have, if they did, "Show Me" would have been a fitting moniker for the people Jesus encountered. People wanted proof. But Jesus was quick to point out, "Unless you see signs and wonders you will not believe." The people wanted to see signs and wonders, and when they did, they believed. But not all who saw or heard would have a deep-rooted, life-altering faith. Some would have more of a temporary moment where their eyes were wowed, but their hearts weren't changed. The official we encounter in today's reading, a government servant who was a person of some influence, seeks out Jesus. He was a desperate parent, and he knew he had no solution to heal his son. So, in faith, he comes to Jesus. Jesus, in His mercy, told the man his son would be healed. Upon hearing that his son had indeed been healed, the official "believed, and all his household" (John 4:53).

Reflection

1. If your faith and/or your relationship with Jesus were represented on a license plate, what would be the phrase people would see?

2. When you think about sharing the gospel with people, being like a worker in a field ready for harvest, what are the fields in your life you need to work?

3. Do you currently live your life as if your present location is the mission field God has for you at this time, or do you just think that you will go on a mission trip at some point in the future?

4. Is your view of God based on what you can see or what you know to be true, even when you can't see it?

Prayer

Pray this simple prayer today:

- Jesus, give me the **eyes** to see the people around me who need to hear my testimony and the goodness of the gospel.
- Jesus, give me your **ears** to listen well and to hear people who are hurting and need a word of kindness and hope shared with them.
- Jesus, give me your **hands** to reach out to people in need and meet them where they are, even if they are different than me.
- Jesus, give me your **heart** to love people and meet their physical needs, so I can share your love and desire to meet their spiritual needs.

Faith on the Mountain

Day 11

John 5:1-29, 30-47

Begin by reading John 5:1-29.

Years ago, I went skiing in Winter Park, Colorado. On one of my first days on the slopes, I was about to get on the chairlift to go all the way to the top of the mountain when another skier caught my attention. There was a man with an orange bib over his ski jacket that read "BLIND SKIER." I was quickly intrigued. I then realized there was another skier with him, a guide to assist. We got on the chair lift and headed to the top of the mountain. I got off first, then watched the blind skier get off and ski to a flat area without issue. I assumed that they would likely take a flatter green trail, but to my amazement, they had a few words and then took off down a more challenging blue trail.

I quickly caught up and skied down behind the blind skier. I watched and listened as the guide skied a bit behind him and called out to the blind skier to orient and make him aware of what was around him. He gave clear verbal calls like, "skier 20 yards on your right", "trees to your left," "turn coming on your right," "slower skiers 50 yards in front of you." I could not believe what I was seeing as the blind skier took on the mountain with no issues and skied down it flawlessly.

When I got to the bottom of the mountain and looked over at the blind skier, do you know what I saw? I saw faith. That man had total faith in the guide who was making his calls. "Now faith is the assurance of things hoped for, the conviction of things not seen" (Hebrews 11:1). He could not see, but he was totally confident in the one leading the way.

In today's reading, we see the third miracle recorded by John: Jesus heals a paralytic at the pool of Bethesda (verses 1-17). We also see that Jesus was growing in popularity and facing opposition. Twice today, we have also seen the words, "Truly, truly, I say to you." This expression appears 25 times in the Gospel of John. This is important because it is a phrase that emphasizes what is being shared. It would be like saying, "I promise, I am telling you the truth" before giving information. Jesus is sharing truth while also sharing things personally from direct knowledge.

With that understanding, we can read verse 24 as, "I am telling you the truth: those who hear Me (Jesus) and believe in Him who sent Me (God) have eternal life. They have already passed from death into life." We see the statement again in verse 25, when Jesus says that the dead will hear His voice and that all who hear will live.

Finish reading John 5:30-47.

Just like those whom Jesus is talking to, many people today search for answers but refuse to go to Jesus for eternal life. They are blind but will not listen to the One who shows the way. Remember that the Bible is 66 books, and they all point to Jesus. He says, *"You searched the Scriptures because you think that in them you have eternal life; and it is they that bear witness about Me."* As we have shared in previous days, faith is a big deal in our relationship with Jesus. Ephesians 2:8-9 says, *"For by grace you have been saved <u>through faith</u>. And this is not your own doing; it is the gift of God, not a result of works, so that no one may boast."*

You likely know what an acrostic is, where you read a word vertically from top to bottom, and a selected letter spells out a word or phrase. I once saw one for FAITH that I think will be helpful as we end our time together today.

FAITH

Forsaking (Abandon, renounce, or give up)

All (The whole quantity, the whole of one's energy or interest)

I (You personally)

Trust (Firm belief in the reliability, truth, ability, or strength of someone or something)

Him (Jesus)

Reflection

1. Like the blind skier, are you confident in the one who is leading the way for you? Will you trust the voice of the Lord, even if you can't always see the path and plan ahead?

2. Because of God's love for humanity, He sent Jesus. And He did this not to condemn us, but to save us. Whoever believes in Christ will not perish but will have eternal life. Is that something that you totally believe? How does it impact your daily life?

3. Where are areas of your faith that you would consider weak? Is there a reason you can identify for that weakness?

Prayer

Ask God to give you full faith that you can trust Him even if you can't see the next steps. Ask Him to remind you that He is fully in control and knows your past, present, and future. This does not mean that you can't ask God questions. He can handle those, but it means you fully trust Him in the unknowns of your life.

Witness to Jesus

Day 12

John 5:30-47

Begin by reading John 5:30-47.

Ever since the television became a common part of American homes in the 1950s, legal dramas starring lawyers, judges, and detectives have been at the core of television entertainment. They began with "Dragnet" (1951), "Perry Mason" (1957), and even "Divorce Court" (1957), becoming weekly occurrences in living rooms across the country. "The Defenders" was part of 1960s television, focusing on a father-and-son attorney duo. Evidence-gathering detectives dominated the 1970s with the introduction of "Columbo," "Kojak," "The Rockford Files," "Starsky & Hutch," and "Hawaii Five-O." The 1980s brought the award-winning "L.A. Law" and even the comedy-drama of "Night Court," which sat in a New York City courtroom after dark. And who could forget Andy Griffith's return to television as "Matlock," a witty, fact-gathering, dramatic courtroom defense attorney. The 1990s brought one of the most successful television franchises ever with "Law & Order," setting the stage for the myriad of legal shows that fill the airwaves and streaming services even to this day.

Over the more than 75 years of television, what each of these shows has in common is the power of eyewitness testimony to make or break a case. Evidence is always important, but a witness can lend credibility to the prosecution or defense, and corroboration is a key part of their testimony. They can say, "I saw it, and this is what happened," as part of their firsthand validation.

In today's reading, we will revisit verses 30-47 from a different angle. In these verses, we hear Jesus talking about being a judge, making judgments, bearing witness, and giving true testimony, which is, of course, legal language. Language that requires a judgment of truth or lies, of innocence or a verdict of guilt. Language is not played out in a courtroom or on a witness stand, but in our own lives.

In the first part of verse 37, Jesus says, "And the Father who sent me has himself borne witness about me." The scriptures, inspired by God, give a firsthand account of who Jesus was, who He is, and who He always will be. When we see Him as the scriptures bear witness, we recognize His divinity and majesty.

The consistent focus of the Christian life for you and me is the daily witness we share as we take up our cross and follow Jesus. John has already used this language, as we go back and look at John 1:34 and again in John 3:32 when John the Baptist serves as a witness for the coming of Jesus. We see it again in John 3:11 as Jesus interacts with Nicodemus, who was trying to figure Jesus out.

The people, as many still do today, are trying to figure out who Jesus is. He continues to tell the crowds that it is not just about what He says, or even what John says, but about what the Father bears witness to and validates in and through Jesus. Like He often does, Jesus points to what those who are committed Jews would know, the Hebrew Bible that you and I today would call the Old Testament. Jesus said, "You search the Scriptures because you think that in them you have eternal life; and it is they that bear witness about me." The Bible is more than a "How-to-Have-Eternal-Life-for-Dummies" that gives instructions to solve our problems.

As we studied yesterday, the Bible points to our provision. Jesus reminds us that the Old Testament scriptures, many of which His audience had spent their lives studying, living out, and teaching to their children, actually point to Him. We see the countless prophecies of His birth, life, work, death, and resurrection.

In His conclusion, Jesus brings the most important leader in Jewish history into the conversation, Moses, the very one who received the

Law directly from God on Mount Sinai (Exodus 19-20). While he did not write about Jesus by name, he wrote of the promised prophet (Deuteronomy 18), the Passover Lamb (Exodus 12), the bronze serpent being lifted up (Numbers 21), and manna from Heaven (Exodus 16), which we will look at more tomorrow. These prophecies, particularly in the first five books of the Bible (the Pentateuch, authored by Moses), lay the theological foundation for the New Testament. And John makes it clear: the scriptures are a witness to Jesus (verse 39), with Moses even writing about Jesus (verse 46).

Reflection

1. When you look at your testimony related to Jesus, what evidence does it show?

2. If your belief in Jesus were put on trial, would there be eyewitnesses to your life that could testify on your behalf?

3. Sometimes "faith on trial" means we are going through difficult times, circumstances, or maybe even persecution for our belief in Jesus. Can you think of a time in the past when that has been true in your life, and how you responded?

Prayer

Ask God to give you a faith that fully believes. A faith that is growing in spiritual maturity and holds on to hope in Jesus in all circumstances and situations. Ask God to give you a desire to read and allow the Word, both the Old and New Testaments, to become a daily part of your life. Share anything you feel like you need to share with God.

The Staff of Life

Day 13

John 6:1-59

Begin by reading John 6:1-15.

John 6 gives us two well-known stories and also the first of what is known as the "I Am" statements in John. Let's begin our time today by looking at what Jesus did with a young boy's lunch.

Sometimes I imagine Jesus smiling as He asked His disciples questions or made statements to them. However, the look on the disciples' faces throughout their time with Jesus probably encompassed every expression one could make. Here, Jesus asks Philip where they should get bread to feed the growing crowd. The crowds were starting to show up because of the things they were hearing about Jesus, His healings, and His teachings. Philip, likely going into a bit of a perplexed panic, says it would take a lot of money to feed a crowd of this size. (The value of two hundred denarii is actually about seven months of wages for a worker.)

Andrew, perhaps in a moment of humor, highlights a boy in attendance who was prepared and had packed a lunch. Barley loaf was common among those of little means, and there is no doubt this boy was an unlikely candidate to solve the day's problems. But limited resources in the hands of a limitless God are a powerful combination.

We see Jesus focusing on people's immediate needs before their spiritual needs. Jesus gives direction, takes the boy's lunch, gives thanks to the Father, and distributes the loaves. He then does the same with the two fish. What happens next is the fourth recorded miracle in John.

With this simple lunch, Jesus provided for five thousand men, and with women and children added, it was likely more than fifteen thousand who ate lunch that day. The people called Him a prophet, but they still did not fully understand who Jesus is. However, they knew there was something different about Him. Jesus removed Himself from the excitement and potential frenzy that was to follow the lunch.

Continue reading John 6:16-21.

Later, in the stillness of the early morning hours, likely between 3 and 6 A.M., the disciples are resting in a boat on the water before a storm pops up, and then they are startled by seeing Jesus walking on the water. This moment is a big deal for many reasons. First, we see throughout the Old Testament that God was over creation, as highlighted in Job 9:8, "who alone stretched out the heavens and trampled the waves of the sea." And here, we see Jesus revealing that He is in full command of the natural elements, which would be another sign of His divinity. This experience, following the earlier feeding of the crowds, strengthened the disciples' belief that Jesus truly was the Messiah. (This story also appears in more detail in Matthew 14:22-36 and Mark 6:45-56 if you would like to read more about it.)

Finish reading John 6:22-59.

This chapter began with barley loaves and ends with Jesus telling the lingering crowd that had tracked Him that He is the Bread of Life (John 6:35). Those in the crowd who were seeking more of Jesus had heard the stories passed down through generations of God providing bread called manna through Moses for forty years in the wilderness (Exodus 16). They wanted their own version of special bread from God. But again, people were thinking with their earthly mindset while Jesus was sharing from a heavenly perspective. He wants to address a hunger that is much deeper than today's meal.

Here, Jesus shares the first of the "I Am" statements. There are seven of these all-important statements found in the book of John:

Seven "I Am" Statements in John

- I Am The Bread Of Life (John 6:35)
- I Am The Light Of The World (John 8:12)
- I Am The Door For The Sheep (John 10:7)
- I Am The Good Shepherd (John 10:11)
- I Am The Resurrection And The Life (John 11:25)
- I Am The Way, The Truth, And The Life (John 14:6)
- I Am The True Vine (John 15:1)

We will look at these statements further over the coming days. Bread is often called the "staff of life" because it is a basic food many associate with sustaining life. Jesus associates Himself with the symbol of bread and declares that anyone who comes to Him will not hunger and anyone who believes in Him will have eternal life.

This is a recurring theme throughout John. It is as if Jesus is saying, "I promise, I am telling you the truth, whoever believes has eternal life," and then, Jesus reaffirms, *"I am the bread of life."* Jesus becomes the spiritual bread by sacrificing His own body and taking on death on the cross. We remember this even today as we observe the Lord's Supper in remembrance of Christ's sacrifice on our behalf.

John 6 is a personal invitation to you and me to come to God's feast. You don't have to bring anything to it, short of yourself, and there is enough for the entire world.

Reflection

1. Do you think more like Philip, overwhelmed by the realities of life, or like Andrew, who brings the lunch to Jesus? What is the difference in those perspectives?

2. What does the story of Jesus walking on the water mean to you?

3. Think about the statement by Jesus, "I am the bread of life." What does that concept of bread mean to you in relation to Jesus?

Prayer

Pray specifically about your relationship with Jesus. If you are not feeling like you are growing in your relationship with Jesus, what might you need to say to Him today? Take some time to say it now. No matter where you are in your relationship with Jesus, He wants you to come to Him, keep your eyes focused on Him, and have your ears open to what He has to say.

Right Time, Right Place

Day 14

John 7:1-24

Begin by reading John 7:1-9.

Have you ever heard sayings like, "You are who you surround yourself with," or "Show me your friends, and I will show you your future"? These short statements highlight the impact the people around you have on you, your development, habits, choices, and mindset. A common term for this is influence. Other people can greatly influence us.

We are usually most influenced by those in closest proximity to us. Young children are most influenced by their parents, while teenagers are increasingly influenced by their friends (hence the term "peer pressure"). I think we would agree that Jesus would be immune from the peer pressure of those He surrounded Himself with. For starters, they all knew He was not like them. This is why they would address him with titles of respect, such as Rabbi (Teacher), Master, or Lord. But we see throughout the Gospel narratives that the disciples often tried to influence Jesus in His decision-making.

We observe the disciples trying to sway Jesus on several occasions, including what we have already seen in John 4, where they tried to get Him to eat the food they picked up in the Samarian town. Elsewhere, we see them asking Jesus questions and making suggestions as they travel together, encouraging Him to stay or go somewhere else. In John 13, we will see strong pushback and a plea from Peter to influence Him when Jesus said He was going to wash the disciples' feet. John does not record the disciples' experience of arguing about greatness and trying to influence Jesus' thoughts, but we see this interaction in each of the Synoptic Gospels.

Remember where we started our time together on Day 1: "But these are written so that you may believe that Jesus is the Christ, the Son of God, and that by believing you may have life in his name." John wants to keep the divine nature of Jesus and His relationship with those who believe central to his Gospel. I hope, as we continue our reading, that you, too, are seeing and believing.

In today's reading, Jesus demonstrates His wisdom as He reveals Himself in yet another example of trusting the Father's timing. But we also see another example of the disciples encouraging Him to get out there more and show the watching world who He really was. The disciples had seen the things Jesus had been doing and heard His teaching; they felt it was time to not hold back any longer. They seemed less concerned about God's timetable. They wanted to get the action going. Much of this is because they still did not fully understand Jesus' mission.

Continue reading John 7:10-24.

Jesus goes to the feast alone, almost in secret, and maybe even a bit incognito, so people would not recognize Him. This was not as much about trying to deceive anyone, as about avoiding the publicity that was quickly growing around Him. Furthermore, some of the religious leaders had begun looking for Jesus in order to have Him arrested. We see that people were divided on who they believed this Jesus was. Ever since Jesus' arrival, there has been division between belief and unbelief, a division still evident today.

While Jesus did not come into town publicly with the rest of His disciples, once He did slip in, He went to the Temple and began teaching again. One thing we see throughout the ministry of Jesus is a boldness to teach in the face of adversity. As we have talked about, He cared deeply about God's timing and about sharing the truth in love. The religious leaders thought that Jesus had not attended the right schools, received the proper training, sat under an appropriate rabbi, attained the necessary credentials, or been part of their holy huddle. Simply put, he was not one of them. Jesus fully agreed and did not try to woo them with what they valued; He simply taught Scripture that they knew, again highlighting Moses. Jesus pointed to the glory and goodness of God, a common part of His public ministry.

Reflection

1. How do you leverage your own influence around you for the sake of the Kingdom?

2. When you hear someone speak, are you more likely to listen to them on the merit of the content they are sharing or the level of their education? How does this view impact your view of Jesus?

3. Can you remember a time you faced opposition because of your beliefs about Jesus or actions as a Christian? Did that experience build your faith or break your faith?

4. Who do you need to share the truth in love with?

Prayer

Spend some time thanking God for the people that are around you in your life, both the people who you influence and those who influence you. Ask Him how you can be not just a bigger influence, but a better influence for God's grace, goodness, and glory. Ask God to give you more people to connect with in your everyday life so that you can hear their story and share yours.

Who Is This Man?

Day 15

John 7:25-52

Begin by reading John 7:25-36.

Have you ever been in a public place and seen someone you thought might be someone you know, but you weren't sure? Most of us have. Maybe you have even had the experience of seeing someone you think *might* even be a celebrity. If you have, and it's been in a public place like an airport or restaurant, then you've likely seen how the presence of the individual in question created a buzz, with some people convinced it is that person, while others are not quite so sure. Sometimes you never really know for sure if you've just seen someone famous or someone who merely *looks* famous.

In today's reading, we begin by jumping back in where Jesus has been teaching in the Temple. There is no doubt that the religious leaders and onlookers are impressed by the knowledge and teaching of this man before them. But as we discussed yesterday, many believed He was not from God and was nothing short of a problem that needed to be addressed. Others are trying to figure out if this man could really be the Christ that they had all been waiting for. They had heard that the religious leaders wanted to dispose of Jesus, but were confused; why did they do nothing if Jesus was just openly teaching in front of them?

Malachi is the last book of the Old Testament before the intertestamental period we discussed on Day 3. Malachi was a prophet who wrote a short four-chapter (only 55 verses) prophetic book that pointed to the promised return of Elijah to prepare the way of the Lord. It is believed that this preparation was fulfilled in the work of John the Baptist before the arrival of Jesus. In Malachi 3:1, the prophet wrote:

"Behold, I send my messenger, and he will prepare the way before me. And the Lord whom you seek will suddenly come to his Temple; and the messenger of the covenant in whom you delight, behold, he is coming, says the LORD of hosts." Because of this, people believed that no one would know where the Messiah would come from, and that he might just mysteriously and magically appear, like some superhero teleported onto the scene. But they thought they knew where Jesus came from, which caused many to struggle with their belief.

As we have seen many times in our readings, Jesus was always protecting God's timetable, but God's plans also protected Jesus. The power was not in those seeking to kill Jesus, even when awareness of Him had been escalated to the chief priests, nor were the Temple police sent to arrest Him. The authority was in God, who is in control of all things at all times; no one could do anything to Jesus until His appointed time. During this time of waiting, people continued to be drawn to His teaching and believed.

Continue reading John 7:37-52.

The "Feast of the Booths" is called *Sukkot* by the Jews. Your Bible translation might even call it the "Feast of Tabernacles." They are all the same festival, which could be considered a fall festival in a church today. It was time to remember the harvest, and it was celebrated over seven days, typically in September or October. Families usually go outside the city and set up temporary shelters, called booths, in remembrance of their ancestors and their 40-year period wandering in the wilderness before they entered the Promised Land. In addition to the seven-day observance of the festival, there is an eighth day, the Great Day, which is a holy day and marks the end of the celebration. Over the first seven days, water is poured on the altar to remember God's provision of water in the wilderness. On the last day, the eighth, water is not poured out, but it is prayed for.

On this Great Day, Jesus followed up by speaking about the same living water He had shared with the Samaritan woman in John 4. John records that Jesus "stood up and cried out," a contrast to other accounts of His teachings and a sign of His great passion for what He was sharing. As the feast was ending, so was His time in Jerusalem until He would return for Passover, His arrest, and crucifixion.

Just as God had provided water in the wilderness, Jesus invites anyone who comes to Him in belief to have their spiritual thirst satisfied, and it will only be satisfied when you come to Him in belief and receive living water. (There is also the promise of the Holy Spirit, but that will not happen until Jesus' appointed time, an arrest, a cross, and an empty tomb.) Some people remained confused and conflicted. Others were merely uneducated about who Jesus was and where He was from. They had already heard he was "Jesus from Nazareth," which was in Galilee, but to be the Messiah, it was known that the promised one would come from the line of David, son of Jesse, who was from Bethlehem in Judea. God, who is in control of all things, used a Roman census to make sure that Jesus was born in Bethlehem, the town that Joseph had to go to register with a very pregnant wife, carrying a special delivery that would take away the sins of the world.

The Temple police did not dare touch Jesus because they realized there was something different about Him and the way He taught. The Pharisee Nicodemus had already interacted with Jesus and was working behind the scenes with his peers to influence them to take a hard look at Jesus. However, again, they would have nothing to do with anyone who threatened their influence or power. A collision was coming.

Reflection

1. Jesus always taught with a boldness that was not intimidated by the threats and security risks. If you had to give yourself a grade 1-100

on your boldness when it comes to your willingness to share about Jesus, what would your grade be?

2. Do you see the power of God in your life and have an understanding that He is in control of all things? Where are areas you need to trust more that He is in control?

3. Have you had the thirst in your life quenched by coming to Jesus in belief? If not, what will it take for you?

4. What is one thing you have been learning this week from your reading in the book of John?

Prayer

Thank God for the goodness of His Word and the opportunity we have to read and study it freely. Ask the Lord to continue to give you a desire to know the Bible, listen to His voice, and a boldness to share the grace of the gospel with others. If you are struggling with believing in Jesus as the promised Messiah, ask God to be gracious with you and continue revealing to you what is true.

Day 16

Light of the World

John 8:1-38

Begin by reading John 8:1-11.

In our first story today, we see a trap set to test Jesus. While Jesus was teaching, the Pharisees brought a woman caught in adultery in front of Jesus (ironically, the man is nowhere to be found, as either he was a part of the scheme or just simply not being charged with the same thing she was). They ask Jesus what they should do, as they were looking for more and more opportunities to trap Him and shut Him up. And at first, Jesus says nothing in response.

The issue is that the decision on her charges would put Jesus in the middle of the Mosaic Law and Roman law. The Pharisees would have upheld the Mosaic Law to stone her, and to let her go would have broken that. But if Jesus says to execute her for the crime of adultery, then He would break Roman law because Rome had taken away the rights for Jews to give official judgment to execute people for religious offenses (remember this for a conversation to come). These religious leaders were likely not looking to determine right and wrong or societal rules, as they had already disregarded the law by failing to bring the man in. They were simply tired of Jesus' teachings and hoped to find something they could charge Him with.

The real issue with these men is that they were quick to see the sin of others but blind to their own. And so Jesus begins writing in the dirt as they push Him further. He finally speaks, but does not say what to do related to either the Mosaic or Roman laws. He simply says that whoever has no sin in their life can throw the first stone. He then goes back to writing in the dirt.

I have always wondered what Jesus was writing in the dirt in front of them. There are many speculations, but no one can know for sure what He wrote or who saw it. Maybe He was writing out their names and a list of their sins, maybe He was writing out Scriptures they would know from the Torah, maybe He was writing a word to the woman, or maybe He was not writing anything relevant at all. The point of this story is not about what Jesus wrote, but a reminder not to judge others when we have sin in our own lives.

Upon hearing Jesus' response, the religious leaders begin leaving oldest to youngest. Either the older men were wiser in this moment, or perhaps they knew they had more sin than others. Some even believed that Jesus had written their names in order on the ground, and it was clear that this moment would not trick Jesus. Once the leaders had all left, Jesus asked the woman where her accusers were. Jesus does not condemn her. But notice that He does give her clear instructions to "go, and from now on, sin no more." This story shows us the incredible compassion and forgiveness Jesus has for people. But it is important to understand there is a difference between condemning and condoning. Jesus did not condone her sin; He forgave her and sent her on with a word to no longer sin.

Continue reading John 8:12-30.

Are you a morning or a night person? That is a preference for most people, but for some, it is more than that. For some, it is a condition called nyctophilia, which is defined as a love of darkness. A nyctophile is someone who feels extreme comfort and freedom in the dark. These people are night people of the highest order, as they want to live and operate in the dark. Jesus shares that there are plenty walking in darkness. As His second "I Am" statement, He says, "I am the light of the world," and that because of Him, people can have the light of life. Some simply live in darkness because they don't know how good it can be to live in the light. If we are not living in Jesus, we are not in the light.

Think about a cave that is full of beautiful formations. Maybe you have been in one before, and it comes to your mind right now. You can't see the beauty of what is there in the dark; you have to bring light to reveal it. The same is true in our lives. The light of Christ begins to reveal the beauty of the life He has intended for you.

Finish reading John 8:31-38.

Jesus addresses a group of Jews who believe He is the Messiah. He uses the word "abide," which we will address more in Chapter 15. It simply means to "live, remain, or dwell" in reference to His word, and this consistency will validate that we are truly His disciples. Jesus is distinguishing between fans and followers. One of the Prince of Darkness's biggest lies is that you will never be free from your past or current realities. However, Jesus leads His followers into freedom.

"The truth will set you free" is likely one of the most quoted phrases, and many likely have no clue that it comes from the Bible. It is found in John 8:32, and the freedom is connected to our abiding in Him and His in us.

Reflection

1. There is no place for judgment for a true Christ follower. How do you avoid judging others and casting a voice of condemnation while also not condoning the sinful actions of others?

2. Remember John talking about bearing witness to Jesus. In today's passage, we now see Jesus bearing witness to the Father. To whom do you bear witness in your daily life?

3. Freedom is waiting for you in Christ. What is holding you back? Why?

Prayer

Ask God to reveal in your life what needs to come into the light. Things you need to find freedom over. God wants to hear from you, so confess as needed. Ask God to give you eyes to see people as He sees them. Ask Him to give you a heart that does not judge people, but freely loves people as He does.

Day 17

The Blind See While Others Are Blind

John 9:1-41

Begin by reading John 9:1-34.

You need light to see. That's not news to you, but do you know how your eye actually works? Our eyes include the cornea, pupil, iris, lens, retina, and optic nerve, which connects them to our brains. These all work together to take the light that enters our cornea and pass it through our pupil, assisted by the iris, which determines how much light is let into the lens. The cornea provides focus, and the retina uses photoreceptors to send electrical signals through the optic nerves to the brain, where they are processed to form what we see. That's an incredibly complex process most of us take for granted every day.

Experts say that approximately 50% of the world's population requires vision correction to see. As our eyes age, they become less flexible, which causes light to focus behind the retina and reduces its effectiveness, leading to vision loss. Spend time with an elderly person, and you may notice their need for more light, especially if they pull out their phone flashlight to see. A 2020 estimate reported that 43 million people worldwide are totally blind.

In today's reading, we see a man for whom any attempt at vision correction by an optometrist will not work, as he has been living in total darkness since birth. As the disciples passed by this blind man, Jesus saw him differently than His followers did. They saw him as a question to be answered, and Jesus saw him as a creation of God to be served. In certain cultures, both in biblical times and today, some people view those afflicted with disorders or disabilities as being cursed or punished for their sins. This tendency was evident among the disciples. Yet Jesus points out that it is not about the man's or his parents' sin; instead, He uses this moment to show that He is the one who can take someone from darkness to light.

Many people had also passed by this man, and now they are interacting with him, but his vision has been restored. This begins an investigation, and the religious leaders, who have again been trying to find a way to get rid of Jesus, do not like that He did this "work" on the Sabbath, a day set aside to be holy, full of rest and a spiritual renewal, and to honor God. However, the leaders had turned the God-ordained day of rest into a legalistic exercise; they had put themselves in the position of making the rules. In this situation, they did not celebrate the miracle; they criticized the moment. Furthermore, they had to do something to cover up the story so as not to lose more followers to Jesus. It is always hard to deny the evidence of a changed life.

Continue reading John 9:35-41.

Jesus circles back to find the man whom He had sent to the pool of Siloam. In this moment, we again see Jesus use the term "Son of Man," the same one He used in John 3 when talking to Nicodemus, to describe Himself. This title refers to the humanity and deity of Jesus, as well as to his humility and to his fulfillment of another Old Testament prophecy in Daniel 7:13-14. The title Son of God clearly points to the deity of Jesus, but Son of Man also focuses on the humanity of Jesus. John later wrote in 1 John 4:2, "Jesus Christ has come in the flesh is from God." Jesus was fully man in the flesh while still being fully God. Philippians 2:6-8 reinforces this while pointing to His humility: "Though he was in the form of God, did not count equality with God a thing to be grasped, but emptied himself, by taking the form of a servant, being born in the likeness of men. And being found in human form, he humbled himself by becoming obedient to the point of death, even death on a cross."

The authority of the Son of Man is referenced multiple times in the Gospels:

- "But that you may know that the Son of Man has authority on earth to forgive sins" - Mark 2:10
- "For the Son of Man came to seek and to save the lost." - Luke 19:10
- "And as they were coming down the mountain, he charged them to tell no one what they had seen, until the Son of Man had risen from the dead." - Mark 9:9
- "And he has given him authority to execute judgment, because he is the Son of Man." - John 5:27
- "Jesus said to him, "You have said so. But I tell you, from now on you will see the Son of Man seated at the right hand of Power and coming on the clouds of heaven." - Matthew 26:64

Jesus asks the question each of us must also answer: "Do you believe?" The man believes in and worships Jesus. Worship is a natural response to our belief. At this moment, Jesus uses sight as a metaphor for our spiritual condition: some find sight (faith), while others remain in blindness (unbelief).

Before we move on, go back to the question the disciples asked: "Who sinned, this man or his parents, that he was born blind?" The truth is, both he and his parents sinned, as you and your parents have also sinned. All humankind is guilty of sin, as Paul tells us in Romans 3:23: "For all have sinned and fall short of the glory of God." We all deserve the punishment that sin requires. This is called the doctrine of original sin, and it is foundational to Christian theology. It means that all of us inherited a sinful nature from Adam, as seen in

Genesis 3. It points not to a single individual's shortcomings but to the spiritual condition of all humanity.

You may feel like it is not fair that Adam's sinful nature has been passed along to you but let us be reminded of another cornerstone of the Christian faith: "But God shows his love for us in that while we were still sinners, Christ died for us" (Romans 5:8). So just as the sinful account of Adam is assigned to each of us, if we believe in Jesus the flawless account of his is freely given to us, giving us life and restoring us in right standing with God.

Reflection

1. When and how did you see God's light for the first time? How has that changed your life since then?

2. What is foundational to your belief in God that you build your life on?

3. Can you think of any blind spots in your Christian life that you need to ask God to work on?

4. How has your belief led to a life of worship?

Prayer

Spend a few moments giving God thanks for opening your eyes to belief. Ask Him to give you a heart that worships daily and a head that believes that He is in control of all things. Consider how you can show more humility, as you see it displayed in Jesus, and ask the Lord to give you a willingness to think of others more highly. Share anything with God as you close your time today.

Sheep and Their Shepherd

Day 18

John 10:1-41

Begin by reading John 10:1-21.

Odds are, you have not spent a lot of time around sheep. If you are one of the rare people who *have* spent time with them, you may know some of the following characteristics:

- Sheep lack a sense of direction.
- They don't carry things on their backs well.
- They can get stuck on their backs if they fall over.
- Sheep are helpless and cannot care for themselves if they are wounded.
- Sheep are emotionally complex with distinct personalities.
- They are highly social animals.
- Sheep recognize their master's voice and will follow it.
- They can't clean themselves and must rely on the shepherd to be cleaned.

Does that list sound like humans at all? In Chapter 10, Jesus talks about sheep recognizing the shepherd's voice, which evidently confuses the people listening. And then, in the middle of His teaching, He gives us the third "I Am" statement, as He calls Himself the door. He has been talking about sheep entering a gate where they are presumed to find safety, but Jesus makes it very clear that He is the door, and anyone who enters by Him will be saved. This is another "follow Me" moment from Jesus. He is pointing to Himself as the Good Shepherd who will lay His life down for all of us.

In verse 14, we see the fifth "I Am" statement when Jesus says, *"I am the good shepherd."* But it is so important that we don't miss the rest of that verse as it continues, *"I know my own and my own know me."* Just like the characteristics of the sheep highlighted above, we must recognize the voice of our Master and follow Him.

The Old Testament prophet Isaiah wrote, "All we like sheep have gone astray; we have turned—every one—to his own way; and the LORD has laid on him the iniquity of us all" (Isaiah 53:6). As we do some self-examination, it is good to reflect on the ways we have gone away from the path and the one who shows the right direction. Do we have patterns and plans in our lives that we chose ourselves? Like the sheep, when we do, we will find problems in this life, as we are helpless to life's wounds and can often get stuck when we fall. But, praise God, He provided the Good Shepherd in Jesus, who came and called us to be His own. "The thief comes only to steal and kill and destroy. I came that they may have life and have it abundantly" (John 10:10). Jesus wants you to know Him and go with Him. When we do, we will experience the life God has intended for us.

Continue reading John 10:22-41.

In verses 22–41, we find Jesus back in Jerusalem during the Feast of Dedication, also known as Hanukkah. Once again, the religious leaders surround Him, demanding a straight answer: "If you are the Christ, tell us plainly." But Jesus has already told them through His words and works. They just refuse to believe. Jesus reminds them that His sheep hear His voice and follow Him, and He gives them a promise that should still bring peace to us today: "No one will snatch them out of My hand."

What comfort we have in knowing that once we belong to the Good Shepherd, our salvation is secure. Even as opposition rises and stones are lifted against Him, Jesus calmly continues His Father's work. The Shepherd who lays down His life for His sheep also holds them fast, unshakable, unlosable, and eternally His.

Reflection

1. Are there any of the characteristics listed of sheep that you can personally identify with?

2. Do you recognize the voice of Jesus when He speaks? Do you value His voice more than you value the voice of culture or your own?

3. When you examine your life, do you think you are currently experiencing the life Jesus intends for you? If not, what is holding you back?

Prayer

Ask God to give you ears to hear His voice more clearly in a very cluttered, noisy world. If there are obvious things that you think are keeping you from that, confess those and ask God to free you from those burdens. If you have places in your life where you feel wounded, or even fallen, ask God to take those from you and provide the healing you need. Ask Him to pick you back up and put you on the right path.

1+1 = One

Day 19

John 10:22-42

Begin by reading John 10:22-30.

If you have ever been to a wedding, you likely have witnessed the main elements of the ceremony: the processional of the family, the wedding party, and, ultimately, the bride. You've also likely sat under the welcome and remarks of the officiating minister, listened to a call to the reading of Scripture, a prayer, the exchanging of the vows, and the rings. This is often followed by the announcement of the new couple ("I am happy to introduce you to Mr. and Mrs. Jeffery Glenn Davis"), then the processional, and, hopefully, instructions for a reception with delicious food. During this time or leading up to a wedding, you may also hear this statement about "two becoming one." That statement signifies a new couple whose lives become a unified partnership, with a shared identity and intimacy in their relationship.

In today's reading, we see Jesus still visiting the Temple during the Feast of Dedication (Hanukkah), an eight-day celebration held in late fall. Hanukkah means "dedication," commemorating the rededication of the Temple in 164 BC after the Maccabean revolt. According to later Jewish tradition, when the Temple was cleansed, there was only enough consecrated oil to keep the seven-branched Temple menorah lit for one day, but the oil miraculously lasted eight days. Today, Hanukkah is celebrated with a nine-branched menorah (a hanukkiah), with eight candles lit over eight nights, using the middle candle (the shammash) to light the others as a remembrance of God's provision and presence.

The Feast of Dedication would be a sacred time for Jewish people, a time to remember God's faithfulness through war and persecution and His promise to send the Messiah from the lineage of David. So, with that backdrop, Jesus answers the question of the Jews around him, "How long will you keep us in suspense? If you are the Christ, tell us plainly." Jesus lets them know that He has already clearly told them, but they decided not to believe and even blame Jesus for their unbelief. It has been two months since the events of verse 21 and Jesus' sharing with them about sheep and a shepherd, but He returns to those references, saying that His sheep will hear His voice, follow Him, and He will give them eternal life. Then He elevates the moment once more, saying, "I and the Father are one." Like a married couple who are two separate people but have a unified partnership and shared identity, Jesus claims this with God. Here, He makes a clear claim of divinity, sharing equality with God.

Continue reading John 10:31-42.

This claim of deity is considered blasphemy to those listening to Jesus. Which is odd, because they had just asked Him to share the truth with them. But when He does, they don't want to believe, but clearly understand the claim that Jesus was making, and therefore want to kill him. Jesus was not politicking and positioning himself to be equal with God; He had already been that from the beginning. Jesus calmly points to the evidence of His life and the Scripture that they would know well, "and Scripture cannot be broken."

The power is not in the words; the power is in the Word and the One who has the authority to validate the declaration. Much like a king who issues a decree, the power lies in the absolute authority that is backed by the king's divine right to issue it. Words can be hollow if not backed by the king. The Word you hold in your hand is invaluable because it is not only inspired by the King of Kings, but it is backed by the Lord of Lords, who has supreme power and absolute authority.

Reflection

1. Wedding bands are the traditional symbol of a married couple. They don't make the people married, but they are an outward symbol of the covenant of marriage. As a believer, an outward symbol of your belief is baptism, and the evidence of your belief is the fruit of your life. Has this been a reality in your life?

2. Has your identity become one with Jesus, where you have aligned your life, will, and possessions with Him?

3. If someone said to you that Jesus never claimed to be from God, what would you say to them?

4. How do you view Scripture? What presence does it have in your life?

Prayer

Ask God to give you a deep love for His Word, making it a part of your daily life. Tell Jesus you want to increase your intimacy with Him. You want to know Him better as you spend more and more time in a relationship with Him. Your faith is personal, but it is not intended to be private. Ask God to continue to allow you to reflect Him to the world around you. Invite Him to reveal to you what needs to change.

Grave Robber

Day 20

John 11:1-57

Begin by reading John 11:1-16.

I am guessing that, at some point in your life, you have been to a funeral. Maybe it was a friend, family member, or someone with whom you or your family had a relationship. In John 11, we see a man named Lazarus (with whom, along with his two sisters, Mary and Martha, Jesus has had a long friendship) fall ill and die. Jesus is not quick to leave His other work and actually says that the reason is not that He does not love His friend Lazarus, but "it is for the glory of God, so that the Son of God may be glorified through it" (vs 4). After being questioned by the disciples, He again highlights the difference between walking in the light and in the dark. This is a concept that should not be new to the disciples or us from our study of John.

Continue reading John 11:17-37.

Here, the story moves along, and Jesus shares the fifth "I Am" statement: "I am the resurrection and the life." He then shares with Martha, "Whoever believes in me, though he die, yet shall he live, and everyone who lives and believes in me shall never die." This thought can be confusing and hard to understand as we think about our earthly bodies, but again, Jesus is communicating an eternal truth.

Jesus then asks an important question that is still asked of you and me today, "Do you believe this?" This is where faith, again, is paramount. We need to understand that faith would not be faith if we fully understood everything. We don't need to understand. We need to trust. I will have plenty of questions to ask God when I am with Him for eternity, but today I just need to believe in order to have open eyes.

Finish reading John 11:38-57.

Now, we see the climax of this story as Jesus, full of emotion, becomes a grave robber in the most unlikely of ways: raising Lazarus from the dead. His sister, Martha, knew that Lazarus was dead, as it had already been four days, but it seems as if Jesus strategically waited to make sure there was no doubt that he was not just sleeping, not merely in need of first aid, not missing a few pieces, not in need of a tune-up. He, in fact, was gone; Lazarus was 100% dead.

Throughout Jesus' life, He models the importance of giving thanks to the Father, and we see that again here. After giving thanks, He calls Lazarus by name and tells him to come out. And Lazarus does! After the miraculous call to life by Jesus, His beloved friend comes out alive, but he is still bound tight in his death wrappings. Jesus has the people around get up close and personal and unwrap him, thus seeing for themselves the reality of Lazarus' new life.

I have always wondered why Jesus has the others get involved in the process. He obviously could have just had Lazarus bust out on his own, or could have just given the command for the grave wrappings to fall from His friend. However, one thing I have discovered over the years is that, after becoming alive in Christ, one needs a healthy community around them as they lay down old ways and wounds. Here we see a picture of the community playing a role in a new life.

Reflection

1. How do you balance your desire to know and understand with your obedience to trust?

2. Do you remember the time in your life when Jesus called you by name out of your grave?

3. Freedom is found in Christ alone, but living in a healthy biblical community is important to your growth as a disciple of Christ. Do you feel like you are living in a healthy biblical community? Are there changes that you need to make?

Prayer

Spend time asking God to reveal questions you have through either gaining more knowledge or increasing your faith. If you are a Christ follower, share a prayer of thanksgiving to Jesus for robbing your grave of sin and giving you a new life. Ask God to reveal to you people in your biblical community who need encouragement, and maybe even some who need your help to take off their grave clothes and step into the life they have been freed to live.

Day 21

Undefeated

John 12:1-50

Begin by reading John 12:1-36.

Do you know what prophecies are? Simply defined, they are predictions of what will happen in the future. They have a bit more depth than just picking the Super Bowl or World Series champs. It would be cool to pick the Super Bowl winners before the game, and a bit more challenging to pick the winner before the start of the season. But we should be able to agree that it would be very impressive if someone picked the Super Bowl winner before that team even existed.

Statistically, most people who pick game winners rarely have a long-term winning percentage above 56%. Let's think of this from a baseball perspective and, rather than picking an outcome, let's talk about producing on the field. A Major League Baseball team takes the field in the regular season 162 times. Have you ever heard of a team having 162 wins and ZERO losses? That has never happened. The 1906 Chicago Cubs and 2001 Seattle Mariners have had the most wins in history, going 116-36 and 116-42, respectively. If, as a batter, you go to the plate 10 times and get a hit 3-4 times, you will be an All-Star player. You can strike out 6 times and still be considered an all-time great.

But what about Jesus? How many Old Testament prophecies are there, and how many did Jesus fulfill? The first part of this question is difficult to answer with precision because there are various speculations about how many prophecies there are about the Messiah in the first 39 books of the Bible. Those are divided into the Pentateuch, the historical books, the wisdom books, and the prophets. Throughout those writings, there are clear prophecies and predictions concerning the coming Messiah. Some scholars may consider a single verse to be prophecy, while others may view the passage as two to three independent prophecies rather than one. And then, do you count repeated prophecies? Because of these views, scholars' counts can vary. Most believe that there are somewhere between 200 and 500 prophecies in the Old Testament pointing to the coming Messiah.

Now, to the second part of the question, how many did Jesus fulfill? Regardless of how one does their count, Jesus fulfilled ALL OF THEM. There are no prophecies in the Old Testament that He failed to fulfill. This means that long before He was physically on Earth, predictions were made, and He fulfilled 100% of them. Unlike the best baseball team ever, Jesus goes undefeated. He is a perfect 10 for 10 with no strikeouts when it comes to prophecies pointing to Him.

Anyone can make predictions and maybe have a good run, but prophecies being fulfilled are so much more, especially when they were recorded thousands of years ago. A professor at Westmont College in California used 600 of his students to calculate the probability that one man would fulfill the major prophecies about the Messiah. They looked at just 48 of the prophecies, and their calculations determined that, for one person to fulfill all of these prophecies, the probability would be 10 to the 157th power. That is a number that contains 157 zeroes! It would be thousands more zeros if the review expanded to the 200 to 500 accepted prophecies. Upon conclusion of the work, the professor declared, "Any man who rejects Christ as the Son of God is rejecting a fact, proved perhaps more absolutely than any other fact in the world."

Here in John 12, we see Jesus increasingly talking about His time on Earth coming to an end. We also see the Pharisees growing more agitated with the loss of followers and influence. Because of the miraculous signs Jesus performed, including raising Lazarus from the dead, even more people have begun to believe and follow Jesus. A collision is coming, but He heads into Jerusalem, as Zechariah 9:9 prophesied, riding on a donkey into what will be called the Holy Week, or the Passion Week. This is the last week of Jesus' life before the crucifixion. In verse 32, we read, "And I, when I am lifted up from the earth, will draw all people to myself." Jesus is referring to the death He will soon take on the cross.

Continue reading John 12:44-50.

Jesus continues to remind all who would listen why He left the right hand of God. "I have come into the world as light, so that whoever believes in Me may not remain in darkness. If anyone hears My words and does not keep them, I do not judge him; for I did not come to judge the world but to save the world" (John 12:46-47). Death by crucifixion was an execution method designed by the Romans for murderers, thieves, and those committing other serious crimes. Jesus, an innocent man, became the ultimate sacrifice and, therefore, became the Savior for all who believe. His death was prophesied in the Old Testament hundreds of years before He was crucified, and perhaps the craziest thing is that crucifixion had not yet even been invented.

Reflection

1. Verse 43 talks about people loving the glory that comes from man more than the glory that comes from God. Who do you find your approval from: people or God?

2. What does it do for your faith in Jesus to know that there is not one prophecy He did not fulfill?

3. Jesus was lifted up when He took on the cross for our sins, and through this, He would draw all people to Himself. How can we continue to lift up Jesus today by glorifying Him with our words and actions so the whole world may see His goodness and grace?

Prayer

Again, thank God for the forgiveness of your sin through Jesus being lifted up on the cross freely and in submission to the Father. Every sin you ever committed was pardoned because of Jesus' innocence, replacing your guilt. Praise God for the amazing grace that saved us. Ask God to reveal to you the areas of your life that are still in darkness and need to come into the light.

Day 22

What's Love Got to Do with It

John 13:1-38

Begin by reading John 13:1-20.

In John 13, we see the final time Jesus spends with His disciples before He is seized by soldiers in the Garden of Gethsemane, just outside the city. He has one last intimate moment with His followers in a borrowed upper room in Jerusalem. This is the holy city where Jesus had been coming since He was a child, but this week is different from all the others. His time is now quickly approaching, and He sill be completing the mission that the Father laid out before Him. But before that, He shares an amazing lesson with the disciples.

When Jesus washes the disciples' feet, it is not merely about the physical act of foot washing. This action we see from Jesus is an example of sacrificial serving. He modeled it throughout His life. The Apostle Paul clearly points to this in Philippians 2:4-11:

> *Let each of you look not only to his own interests, but also to the interests of others. Have this mind among yourselves, which is yours in Christ Jesus, who, though He was in the form of God, did not count equality with God a thing to be grasped, but emptied Himself, by taking the form of a servant, being born in the likeness of men. And being found in human form, He humbled Himself by becoming obedient to the point of death, even death on a cross. Therefore God has highly exalted Him and bestowed on Him the name that is above every name, so that at the name of Jesus every knee should bow, in heaven and on Earth and under*

the Earth, and every tongue confess that Jesus Christ is Lord, to the glory of God the Father.

Continue reading John 13:21-38.

John 13:34 points to a new commandment, "That you love one another: just as I have loved you, you also are to love one another." The Greek word used in this passage for "new" would be used to describe freshness, or the opposite of worn. The truth of this commandment is being presented in a fresh way. In the Old Testament, it was known that people should love their neighbors, but in this new display and new command, it extends beyond just loving our neighbors as ourselves. It calls us to love our neighbors better than ourselves. Love becomes the defining mark of a true believer. Everything we say and do is useless if there is no love behind it.

In the 1960s, on the south side of Chicago, a parish priest at St. Brendan's, Peter Scholtes, led a youth choir that met in the church basement. They were to lead services for upcoming ecumenical (representing numerous different Christian churches) and interracial events. He began looking for the perfect song for these events, but upon searching, he could not find what he felt needed to be communicated. So, he wrote in a single day what has now become the famous hymn, *"They Will Know We Are Christians by Our Love."*

"By this all people will know that you are My disciples, if you have love for one another." It is not by our Christian apparel, our stickers, our church cheers, our church membership, the knowledge we have gained, or our Christian lingo. It is also not by what we refrain from doing. According to Jesus, it is simply love that will be the distinguishing trait for those who call themselves Christ followers.

If you want to live differently, love differently. When you shine and show that love, you will have one of the greatest evangelistic tools available to you today. People are attracted to love because we all desire it.

Reflection

1. Think on the passage from Philippians 2 above. We often decide that we want to be in control, we want to be king, we count not only equality with God, but sometimes, in our actions, superiority to God. We too often fill ourselves up rather than empty ourselves. Do you resonate with that struggle or not?

2. Jesus was always obedient to God's plan. Is that your story? Are you willing to live in submission to God's plan for your life?

3. Do a little love test on your life. When you truly love someone, you often are willing to put it on the biggest billboard you can get, write it in the sky, or include it in your social media. When you consider the billboard of your life, is love showing up on it?

Prayer

"Jesus, you are my everything." Focus your prayer today simply on telling Jesus you love Him. Share with Him why you love Him and ask Him to grow your love for him as well as for those around you. Give

Jesus the honor and recognition that belongs to His name. Tell Him that His name is above every other name in your life and that you not only confess that He is Lord, but you want your life to bring glory to the Father through how you publicly express your love for Jesus and others.

Day 23 One Way Up

John 14:1-21

Begin by reading John 14:1-14.

Mount Everest is the tallest mountain in the world at 29,032 feet. It is very dangerous to reach the top, and only a few skilled climbers attempt it each year. There are several routes to the summit, including the South Col, Northeast Ridge, West Ridge Direct, and Fantasy Ridge. These are just a few of the estimated 20 routes one may take, with most climbers using the two easiest.

Much of life is similar to this; there are different ways to the same destination. While you and I will likely never summit Mount Everest, maybe there are other mountains you've been to that you could think about. Maybe you approached from the East or West, while others can get there from the North or South. Unfortunately, some people think it is like this with God. He sits on top of the mountain, and there are many different ways to get to Him. In this thinking, some may be working their way up to God by being a good Muslim, or others through faithfully committing to Hinduism, Judaism, Shintoism, a Chinese or African traditional religion, or even some view being a Christian as one of the routes to work their way up to God. The thought is that as long as we are all committed to our faith and believe in God, we will all get there one day through the route we are taking. This concept is called universalism.

However, according to John 14:6, this is wrong and, unfortunately for so many, a sad trap. "I am the way, and the truth, and the life. No one comes to the Father except through me." Those are the words of Jesus. He is telling all of us that there is no other route to God but through Him.

Here is another way to consider this. Think about all the things in your life that require a passcode. A few that quickly come to mind may be your phone, computer, WiFi, tablet, TV, bank account, and, for some, even your front door. Jesus makes it clear that to enter Heaven, it is through just one passcode. That is simply Him and Him alone. That is the one way for you and all the world to spend eternity in the presence of God rather than being cast out in judgment.

If you view God as sitting atop a mountain, He did not have to create a way for anyone to reach Him, but in His love, He did. I have heard some say that it's not fair for a loving God not to accept ALL people, but again, Jesus continues to tell us that God will accept ANYONE who bears the mark of His name. And if someone gets upset with you about that, you just have to point to Jesus, since you didn't say it. He did. As many have said, including the famous English preacher Charles Spurgeon, we have a great need for Christ, and thankfully, we have a great Christ for our need.

Continue reading John 14:15-21.

Here, Jesus promises the Holy Spirit to come in His physical absence. In different translations, we see different descriptive words used for the Holy Spirit, including "Helper" (ESV, NKJV), "Counselor" to be with you forever (CSB), "Advocate" to help you (NIV, NLT), and even the Message translation (which is a paraphrase of the Bible) uses the word "Friend" so that you will always have someone with you. The Greek word here is "paraclete," which describes the Holy Spirit as advocate, counselor, or comforter. Jesus would soon leave and go to Heaven, but in His departure, He promised never to leave us, as the Holy Spirit will be with us as our paraclete, advocate, counselor, helper, and friend.

Jesus reminded His followers not to "let their hearts be troubled or afraid because He was with them. If Jesus stayed with us physically, He may be able to be with some believers sometimes, or even many believers many times, but because He left to prepare a place for us, and the Holy Spirit was given to us, He can be with ALL believers ALL the time!

Chapter 14 begins the Farewell Discourse and runs through Chapter 17. Jesus is teaching His followers for the last time, as His death, resurrection, and then ascension are quickly approaching. This discourse, recorded by John, who would have been in the room, is given by Jesus to His disciples immediately at the end of the Last Supper in Jerusalem, the night before heading to the Mount of Olives, where He will be arrested.

Reflection

1. At the beginning of John 14, Jesus says, *"Let not your hearts be troubled. Believe in God; believe also in Me."* He then tells His disciples that He is going to prepare a place for them and that He will come again to take them there. When you think about that, what thoughts come to your mind?

2. Think about each description found in John 14:16. Jesus is the Way. Jesus is the Truth. Jesus is the Life. Now, take it one step further and personalize it. Jesus is my Way. Jesus is my Truth. Jesus is my Life. Are those realities you are experiencing every day?

3. When you think about the presence of the Holy Spirit in your life, do these words describe the relationship you have – Helper, Advocate, Counselor, Comforter, and Friend?

Prayer

Recognize and tell God that, apart from Him, your life is hopeless. Thank God, who is rich in mercy, for sending His very own Son, giving your life purpose and meaning. Praise Jesus, who lived a life you could not live and died a death He did not deserve, so that you could one day be with Him and the Father. This is a prayer that should be on our lips and in our hearts daily. Don't allow your salvation to become so common that it does not leave you awestruck with how amazing the grace and goodness of God are toward you. Even after He gave us Jesus, in His kindness, He also gave us the Holy Spirit for the rest of time on this Earth. That is truly Christ in you, the Hope of Glory.

Day 24 Vine and Branches

John 15:1-27, 16:25-33

Begin by reading John 15:1-17.

Do you use the word "abide" regularly? I'm guessing it's not one you use in your daily vocabulary. This word, "abide," appears 40 times in the Gospel of John, and we see 10 of those here in our reading today. So, what does it mean to abide? To abide is to remain, stay, or dwell; it could even mean "to be present." It is a command that Jesus used often.

In John 15, along with the call to abide, we see Jesus share the seventh "I Am" statement, "I am the vine." As part of the farewell discourse we introduced earlier, Jesus continues to share with His disciples before His arrest. He uses an illustration of a vine, branches, and fruit, not to highlight the grapes, olives, or grains that are easily grown in that climate, but to demonstrate our relationship with Him. For us to be in a right relationship with Him, we must remain, stay, dwell, or be present with Jesus. He is the vine, and we are the branches.

Like this picture that Jesus shares, we need to be reminded of where we should be. If you cut off a branch from the vine, it has no use and will, in time, wither and die. Jesus holds all things together. I once heard it said that abiding is not just about our place but our posture, not how we sit in a chair, but how we approach Jesus.

Another book that the apostle John wrote is the book of Revelation. This book, a record of a vision God gave John, records Jesus addressing the church in Laodicea, one of the seven churches in modern-day Asia Minor, now part of Türkiye. There, Jesus says, "Behold, I stand at the door and knock. If anyone hears my voice and opens the door, I will come in to him and eat with him, and he with me" (Revelation 3:20).

This picture of a door shows that when we become a Christ follower, Jesus comes and dwells in us. In that moment of opening our life to Him, we receive by believing and begin to live by trusting that Jesus is everything we need.

Jesus remains in us, and we must remain in Him, a mutual dwelling together. Abiding in Him has to become a continual, daily process. You will be tested, but standing firm and remaining steadfast with Jesus will not only produce fruit but also more faith.

Jesus says that one of the fruits of our faith is obedience. While your salvation became secure upon your confession of faith and your promise to Jesus as Lord of your life, you now must move from confession to commitment. Action must follow awareness.

Continue reading John 15:18-27.

Jesus shifts here from talking about love to addressing hate. Our goal, obviously, should not be to have people hate us. But Jesus wants all His followers to know that He is divisive. He was then, and He still is today. Years ago, I traveled to India and, while there, learned more about the Hindu faith, a polytheistic religion. Hindus have varied beliefs, ranging from one god to 33 gods to over 330 million gods. I quickly realized that when someone talks about "god," there is rarely a problem because of the widespread definition of "god." But when someone talks about Jesus, there is often a real problem. That name was a divider for me when I was there, and it remains a divider wherever you travel in the world.

Jesus reminds His followers in John 15 that many in the world will reject Him and the one true God, but that will also be true of those of us who are His followers. A danger you may face is that in the past, you may have been told that if you give your life to Jesus, there is a list of incredible things you will receive with this new life in Him. While this is, of course, true, if that's all we pay attention to, we're not fully counting the cost of being a disciple of Jesus. The goodness and grace of God are amazing and can bring purpose and passion, but if you are not prepared in advance, you will likely struggle when opposition to your faith arises. When we live in the call of John 15, the world should see our fruit, and I am confident that opposition will come in time. However, there is hope. If we remain faithful in Christ, we can have peace because He has overcome the world.

Finish reading John 16:25-33.

In this passage, the hour has now come when Jesus' followers will soon scatter, and the next day, Jesus will be standing alone before Pontius Pilate, the Roman prefect (what we would call a governor) of Judea in Jerusalem. The storm clouds are becoming thicker, and it looks like tribulation is coming. But actually, triumph is on the horizon.

Reflection

1. Do you feel like you are actively abiding in the vine?

2. What fruit do you think God wants you to bear in your life?

3. Listening to the wrong people will leave you in the wrong places. How do we make sure we listen to the right people so we can be in the right place with the right posture toward God?

4. Are you prepared for any persecution you may face in this world? A good question to ask yourself is, "Would I rather be an outcast now or cast out later?"

Prayer

Ask God to continue to grow the fruit of faith in your life. Jesus knows your name, and He knows your need. Spend time praying and, even though He knows your needs, articulate those to Him today. Ask Jesus to give you strength and courage for any persecution that may come because of your faith. May the Lord prepare your faith today for whatever tomorrow brings. I had a friend who ended prayers like this, and I think it may be appropriate for your prayer today. "Jesus, Your will, Your way. Nothing more, nothing less. Amen."

Day 25 The Promised Gift

John 16:1-15

Begin by reading John 16:1-4a.

Jesus is again bringing the conversation in this upper room back to the reality that the end of His time with his friends is quickly approaching. Part of His final warning is to prepare His followers for the coming persecution that they will face because of their association with Him. A part of this opposition will be them not only being cast out of their places of worship and societal status, but also being killed. As we see more of their stories, we see they have moments of fear, but after seeing a risen Jesus again, they move forward in faith, even in light of these risks.

As we have already discovered, Jesus is a divider amongst men, and He even knows that some people will kill true Christ-followers, believing they are actually serving God. We see this in Acts as Stephen is killed, becoming the first Christian martyr, with Paul watching as he seeks out official papers to pursue and kill Christians. This has continued to happen over the last 2000 years. Even today, we see Christian brothers and sisters being killed for their faith in parts of Africa and Asia, where official state religions allow for other religions in their service to a false god, to persecute, and even kill those who claim belief and allegiance to Jesus.

Continue reading John 16:4b-15.

Jesus is reminding His followers and us that our hope is in Him. Both Peter (John 13:36) and Thomas (John 14:5) had previously asked Jesus where He was going as He began talking more about completing His mission. Here, Jesus is sharing more about the reality of what is coming for those who are left behind, rather than about the destination He is going to. He knows that the sorrow of the moment will not last forever, but the reality of the mission that they are a part of will be made clear. Just as He said in John 14, Jesus highlights that the Holy Spirit will come and be with them, as well as fulfill His role of convicting people of sin, revealing God's glory, righteousness, and judgment, both for those who believe and for those who do not. The role of the Holy Spirit is not just to bring guilt to sinful people, but more of a divine awakening to one's spiritual condition falling short of the standard of a Holy God that leads to repentance, a growing relationship with God through the saving grace of Jesus, and real and recognizable evidence of a transformed life.

Have you ever been given a gift that you just did not know what to do with? I am not just talking about a bad gift, but about something odd that makes you wonder what the giver was thinking. When I was a kid, I received one from my grandfather. Now, the context is that he grew up during the Great Depression, was part of the Greatest Generation, serving in Europe during World War 2, and had a career as a police detective. My excitement on Christmas morning was soon replaced with a puzzled feeling on Christmas afternoon. As I opened gifts, I got to the one he had given me and, taking off the wrapping paper, saw a nice box that said, "Three Gold Oak Hangers." My first thought was that it was a borrowed box, and no telling what exciting thing might be waiting for me inside. As I opened the box, to my surprise, I found two pant hangers inside. I looked at the front again and told my father one was missing, then asked what I was to do with the pant hangers. It made my parents laugh, but I was still confused about the gift and why it wasn't even the right number.

Later that afternoon, we called my grandparents to check in, as many do on holidays. I thanked them for the gifts and then asked, "I don't know if you guys know, but the box was wrong because it said there were supposed to be three hangers in it." My grandmother spoke up, saying that my grandfather liked them so much that he kept one for himself. I did not really use that gift; I just put it in the closet because it was not very exciting for a kid. When my grandfather died, we were at their house doing some things, and I heard my dad yell from my grandfather's bedroom, "You can come in here and get your other hanger." Ironically, I don't have those hangers anymore, but I still have the box and keep pictures and things in it. A gift that is never used has little value to anyone.

Just as Jesus promised to the disciples, you and I have been given the gift of the Holy Spirit living in us and working through us. As we also read in John 14, the Holy Spirit is the helper we need, but also the Spirit of Truth. God graciously gave us Jesus for 33.5 years, who took on the cross for you and me, but in His overflowing and unmerited favor, He gave us the Holy Spirit for the rest of our days on this Earth.

Reflection

1. Do you ever think and pray for Christians around the world who are living in regions where they may be persecuted and even killed for their faith? What action might this knowledge call you to?

2. Jesus shared that He was going to the one who sent Him because His mission was about to be completed. Have you ever asked God what your mission is on Earth and what completion looks like?

3. Jesus gave His friends in the upper room reassurance about the coming of the Holy Spirit. How does this promise make you feel today?

4. When you consider the gift of the Holy Spirit in your life, is this a gift you are allowing to be spoken daily in your life, or have you treated it like something given to you but never used?

Prayer

Begin your time by praying for persecuted brothers and sisters of the faith around the world. Ask the Lord to not only provide and protect them, but to give them the courage to face the opposition that comes their way. Ask the Lord to give you the same type of unwavering faith. Thank the Lord for the provision and presence of the Holy Spirit in your life. Invite the Holy Spirit to reveal things to you today that need to change or people that you need to share a word of hope with.

Day 26 Overcoming the World

John 16:16-33

Begin by reading John 16:16-24.

Jesus' tone has changed as He knows He is getting closer and closer to the cross. The disciples, however, are unaware that He is just a few hours away from being arrested later in the evening. They will never be with Him like this again, this side of the crucifixion. However, it is likely that after three years together, they could sense the seriousness in Jesus' voice.

They were confused and troubled by the Master's words and seemed to be engaged in side conversations again, trying to figure them out. Jesus was not only trying to prepare their minds for the gap in His physical presence but also to prepare their hearts for what was on the horizon. He knew that very difficult days were coming.

When one is not prepared for a crisis, it can lead to feelings of overwhelming fear, poor decision-making, loss of rational thought, panic, or even the physiological "fight-or-flight" response. Jesus wanted to reassure the disciples that when the panic set in and it felt like everything was out of control, it was just for a short period, as their sorrow would soon be turned to joy. While Jesus enjoyed the fellowship with His friends over the years, He knew He would have to walk these last steps alone.

Continue reading John 16:25-33.

Jesus begins closing His farewell discourse with the disciples, reminding them in these final moments together of a few important thoughts to hold on to. First, the Father loves them. Secondly, Jesus had come from heaven, born as a human, and now would die and rise again to be with the Father, completing the mission set before Him. And finally, He speaks clearly to them that He has overcome the world. He uses here the Greek word *nikos*, which translates to "overcome," meaning to defeat, or to win a "victory" over, as in a conquest or even like a military conflict. (This is also where the most recognizable brand in the world, with its iconic swoosh logo, NIKE, gets its name.) Jesus is reminding those He deeply loves that they may have peace, not from the storm, but in the storm.

Everyone, at some point, will face storms of sorrow, intense suffering, agonizing pain, and even the sting of loss. These emotional realities are a part of living and loving people. If that has not been true for you yet, I promise you they will knock on your door at some point along the way. Jesus wants you to know what He wanted His disciples to know: that we can take heart as Jesus has victory over difficult times, affliction, hardship, trouble, sin, and even death!

My friend Jonathan understood and embraced this truth. He dedicated his life in faithfulness to God, had an unyielding commitment to the Great Commission, and held on to the hope of Jesus in both life and death. After years of leveraging his life for the sake of the gospel all over the world, he and his family took a step of faith to share the same passion and purpose for gospel advancement through a local church. During that time, Jonathan was diagnosed with a brain tumor. For the next six years, he battled cancer until, ultimately, he succumbed to the disease at just 43 years of age. In the last days of his life, I sat by his bed in moments of silence and discussion. At one point, he reached over and grabbed my arm as he thought about what he knew was his coming death and said, "God is good and can be trusted." That does not feel like a statement that someone makes as they are losing their battle with cancer unless they know that the VICTORY has already been won.

Jonathan knew that just as Jesus was getting ready to leave this world, so was he. He was not leaving the world in defeat, but in victory, because he believed in Jesus. Jonathan knew the deep peace that Jesus offers each of His followers, a peace that is not defined by our circumstances or troubles. He knew and held to the truth of 2 Corinthians 5:8, that while he would be absent from the body, he would be present with the Lord. We too can be courageous, knowing that Jesus, the author and perfector of our faith, is fully in control in both this life and the next.

Reflection

1. Unfortunately, trouble is a part of life. The question you have to answer is not IF you have hard times, but how you will respond WHEN the hard times come? Will you believe and trust, or be full of fear and panic?

2. Have you experienced God turning sorrow into joy? How has the overcoming power of Jesus grown your faith?

3. In our culture, you have to keep reorienting your eyes and hearts from the fleeting joys of the world to the complete satisfaction that only heaven will provide through the access it offers through belief in Jesus. What today causes you to be distracted from rejoicing always and giving thanks in all circumstances?

4. Does your awareness of God in your daily life produce worship or worry?

Prayer

Thank God for the provision and presence of Jesus in your life. Tell Jesus that you know He has overcome sin and death not just for the entire world, but for you personally. Now you can be courageous, trusting in the victory that has already been won and live in peace regardless of the circumstances that come your way. Ask God to grow a steadfast courage in you and tell Him you trust Him. Ask Him to increase the evidence of that in your daily life. Share anything on your heart.

Day 27

Great Prayers

John 17:1-26

Begin by reading John 17:1-5.

Have you ever been in the presence of someone and wondered how you got into this intimate moment, feeling somewhat like a bystander? When I did a chaplain residency at a hospital, I felt that when I experienced my first death. The patient was an older man, and his entire family was there as he passed. I was the outsider, but my role put me in a room with about 30 family members. After he passed, there was praying, crying, and almost an hour of just singing worship songs together. I had a deep moment with this family as they spoke to their father and grandfather. It was a beautiful thing to experience, and I was thankful that this was the first of its kind in my role.

In today's reading, Jesus transitions from sharing with His friends to having an intimate moment of communication with His Father. Throughout this time, the others in the room were able to simply watch, listen, process, and experience. I am sure that, as my experience in that hospital room marked me, the disciples' experience in the upper room marked them.

Jesus' prayer here is not necessarily superior to other prayers in the Bible, as prayer is not so much about the words spoken as about the heart and intention of the one praying and the attention and affection of the one being prayed to. But in His words, we hear the deep reality of the end coming and Jesus showing honor and respect to the Father.

In the beginning, we see Jesus' physical posture: "lifted up his eyes to heaven," with what seems to be open eyes and obviously not a bowed head. A reminder for us that prayer is much more about the posture of our hearts than about our bodies. Much like we saw yesterday, this is not a moment of defeat but a prayer of accomplished victory.

Jesus again makes a clear claim of deity when He says He has authority over all flesh and emphasizes that He alone can give eternal life. Christ did not just give glory to the Father through obedience on the cross; He glorified God every day. It's a reminder for us as we don't just give honor and glory to God in the big moments of life, but in the step-by-step journey of faith.

Continue reading John 17:6-19.

Jesus made clear the goodness and grace of God, revealing God's character for the world to see. He reflected the Father. In this moment, we see Jesus praying for His friends whom He loved. While Jesus knew what lay ahead for Him, He also understood the reality that awaited them. Just as we read in John 15, when we remain or dwell with God in us, we not only realize His glory but reflect it.

Verses 15-19 are very important for us to reflect on and internalize today. Just as Jesus was not of this world, we too are called to not be of the world. When we become believers in Jesus, God does not just beam us up out of the world to be with Him in heaven; He keeps us in the world to be His ambassador of love, His messenger of grace, and His champion of truth. This mission assignment is for everyone who believes in Jesus and has now found their identity in Him. You should not just be a consumer of the gospel, but also a conduit spreading it to those around you. Like Jesus, reflecting the Father while proclaiming the message of Jesus Christ.

Finish reading John 17:20-26.

Have you ever considered the provision and power of prayer in your life? Prayer is simply talking to God and listening to Him as a part of good two-way communication. In this moment of intimacy with the one who created you and sustains all things, you can experience the joy and depth of what your Christian life could be. If you feel you don't know how to pray or are afraid you will do it wrong, I encourage you to take the pressure off yourself. I am confident you know how to talk to someone. That is a great beginning in your communication with God; just talk to Him. Be simple and honest, as there are no magic words or special formulas for prayer.

God desires to be in a relationship with you, and that was made possible through Jesus reconciling us to Him. When I was younger, I read 1 Thessalonians 5 and the simple instructions of verse 17, "pray without ceasing," and it deeply impacted me. Suppose these are the instructions given to us for our entire days, weeks, months, and years, and that our lives should simply be covered in prayer. We are to be in a consistent conversation and connection with God. This happened as Jesus tore the veil separating God and man, accomplishing the work God gave Him to do. Praying without ceasing is letting your day begin with "Dear God," and end with "Amen."

Jesus finishes His prayer before leaving the upper room, moving to the garden, and His coming betrayal.

Reflection

1. Because of Jesus' work, we have access to God. Have you considered that this is why you can pray in Jesus' name?

2. What distracts you from being in daily communication with God?

3. Do you feel when you pray, they are full of power and faith, or are your prayers laced with unbelief and weakness?

4. Has your communication and relationship with God removed a "me-centric" mindset and replaced it with a big "God-centered" awe and wonder in your life?

Prayer

Read through the Lord's Prayer in Matthew 6:9-13. In it, we see Jesus teaching His followers and giving us a model for prayer. We see worship, a focus on God's will, a request for daily provision, and a focus on forgiveness and protection. You may follow that pattern in your prayer today or pray as you feel directed.

Day 28 Betrayal and Bearing Witness

John 18:1-40

Begin by reading John 18:1-14.

You likely have watched a movie or read a book with a major plot twist at the end, but when you look back, you can see that the clues were there the whole time. That was what these days must have felt like for the disciples. While Jesus was with His disciples over the last three years, He shared with them that this time was coming, but they did not fully understand. Jesus has also already said that He is all about His Father's timing, as clear as can be if we go all the way back to the first miracle John records. When Jesus turns water into wine, He reminds His mother that He is submitted to His Father's timing. That timing brings Him to this moment and this place.

Jesus knows what it's like to be betrayed by a friend. He is betrayed and arrested because the Jewish leadership, who had been working for a long time, finally set their trap and felt like it was foolproof, as they secured one of Jesus' closest friends and followers to help deliver Him in exchange for 30 silver coins. What they don't understand is that they have little control over the situation, as these moments were set generations ago. God is fully in control, even amid their malicious activity.

Continue reading John 18:15-27.

When Peter first interacted with Jesus, he and his brother, Andrew, identified Him as the long-awaited Messiah, and, according to Luke, he got down on his knees before Jesus and said, "Go away from me, Lord, because I am a sinful man" (Luke 5). Peter was a bit impulsive, quick to commit, and often quick to speak up, sometimes without thinking first. He asked countless questions to Jesus and was a key friend to Him. When the disciples saw Jesus walking on the water, Peter got out of the boat and, as he took his eyes off Jesus, he grew scared and began to sink. I am sure that some of the other disciples later gave him a hard time about that moment, but none of them dared to get out of the boat. Just hours earlier, Peter had proclaimed his allegiance to Jesus, telling his friend and Lord that even if he had to die with Him, he would never deny Him.

Peter would go on to preach and teach with great boldness, and, as Jesus had first said, he would become a rock for the early church. But in these moments, he is scared and unsure. After Jesus is arrested and brought before the Jewish leaders, Peter remains close enough to see what is going on while staying at a distance so as not to be found out. He is identified as one who had been with Jesus, but he quickly denies it. And then again. And finally, a third time, and in that moment, the rooster crows, a painful reminder to Peter of his cowardice that Jesus had foretold. Those impulsive denials were likely filled with so many regrets.

Finish reading John 18:28-40.

When Jesus was born, King Herod was the King of Judea and had heard reports of the "King of the Jews" being born. "King" was a title Herod was unwilling to give up or share with anyone, and he asked the wise men who had travelled from distant lands to let him know where Jesus was, because he wanted to find Him, albeit with ulterior motives. He later ended up killing all male children under two years old to protect his power. Now, over the last three years, Jesus' life had been threatened numerous times in the ongoing conflict with religious leaders, who also did not want to lose their power or position.

In response, Jesus had highlighted the Jewish leaders' hypocrisy, greed, misplaced authority, and lack of true care for the people they led and the God they served. This caused them to burn with anger, and it seems to many that the conflict with religious leaders now leads Jesus to this moment. The Pharisees, chief priest, and scribes had accused Jesus of disobeying Mosaic Law and blasphemy. They identified Him as a false prophet, and Caiaphas, the high priest in Jerusalem, had had enough.

But the Jewish leaders did not have the authority to have Jesus put to death in Judea, which was under Roman control. They had to have Pontius Pilate, the Roman governor of the province, agree and authorize Jesus' death. They thought death was the only way to end the distraction.

As we read, Pilate does not want to have anything to do with this and tries to send Jesus back to the Jewish leaders. He feels forced, and in the conversation, Jesus again says that His kingdom is not of this world. He tells Pilate, "For this purpose I was born and for this purpose I have come into the world—to bear witness to the truth." This is missional language as Jesus shares His agenda in response to the questions about being a king.

Jesus is the truest revelation of God, divinity in the flesh, who came with a mission on His mind, given by the Father and faithfully carried out by Him, the Son. Those who trapped Him thought they were in control. Pontius Pilate thinks he has the authoritative control. But there is only One who controls all things and all people.

If someone bears false witness, they knowingly state as fact something that is not true. But Jesus, being fully God and fully man, bears witness to the truth, which means He came to make a statement. God the Father, full of love and grace, through Jesus, delivers people from sin and separation from Himself.

Reflection

1. Betrayal by a friend is an awful thing. If you have experienced it, you know. Why do you think Judas betrayed Jesus?

2. Like Peter, are you ever positioned close enough to know what is going on with Jesus but at a distance where you are less likely to be identified as a follower?

3. Jesus said He was to bear witness about the truth. How can you bear witness about Jesus?

Prayer

Ask God to give you the courage to be a witness of Jesus Christ. Ask Him to help you share freely with people you come in contact with and live a life that bears witness to His goodness and grace. If there have been times when you feel you have fallen short of your witness, maybe even betrayed Jesus in certain moments, ask Him to forgive you for those, and tell Him whatever you want to as you think about your life going forward.

Day 29

Paid in Full

John 19:1-42

Begin by reading John 19:1-37.

In the Old Testament, we see people offering animal sacrifices to God as a temporary payment, or covering, for their sin. It was a symbol of God's justice and His grace. We can see animals being sacrificed for people all the way back to Adam and Eve (Genesis 3:21). When they sinned in the garden, God killed animals in an act of provision for their clothing.

The book of Leviticus, the third book of the Bible, was written by Moses and gives clear instructions on why and how offerings should be made on our behalf to God. It tells us that the life of an animal is in its blood (Leviticus 17:11) and that blood is for the atonement, which means "making amends, making right, or covering up," for those who have sinned. The book of Hebrews says further that, "without the shedding of blood there is no forgiveness of sins" (Hebrews 9:22).

As an offering, someone would bring an animal before God, but not just any animal. A sacrificial animal had to be spotless, or without blemish. The person offering the sacrifice would identify with the animal as a substitute for their sin. The priest would lay his hand on the animal and pray, symbolically transferring the person's sins to the animal. Then the punishment for sin was put onto the animal, which was death and the shedding of its blood. Instead of the person dying for their sins, God provided the animal to take their place for them as a penalty payment. This would be an act that reminded people of the serious nature of sin and its consequences, as it was performed each year as a temporary covering for sins.

Sin is a serious issue to God, and it should be to us as well. The book of Hebrews says that the sacrifices of those animals were insufficient to take away the guilt of our sins forever. The annual offering of animal sacrifices was just a foreshadowing of the perfect and complete sacrifice made by Jesus Christ on the cross. Jesus' death was a once-and-for-all sacrifice that completely satisfies the death our sin owes. Pilate identified that there was no guilt in Jesus. He was right. All the guilt was in humanity. That is why Jesus became a substitute for you and me.

We read in John 19:30, "When Jesus had received the sour wine, He said, 'It is finished,' and He bowed His head and gave up His spirit." What is finished? His life? Yes, His life and work up to that point were finished. But that's not all that was finished. The spiritual battle was over. Sin had been paid for. It was not a pardon on the cross. There was surely payment. The spotless Lamb of God shed His blood on Calvary so that you and I could be free.

One of my favorite words in the Bible comes from this moment: "propitiation." Propitiation is the act of appeasing or satisfying. On the cross, God the Father, in His great mercy, transferred the wrath due to you and me onto His Son, Jesus, thus satisfying the wrath of God against our sin. That is amazing grace!

As one theologian said, "Before we can begin to see the cross as something done for us, we have to see it as something done by us." Jesus lived the life we should have lived and died the death we should have died. Jesus' pain on the cross as He was broken was real, but He did not look merely to the cross, but beyond. The Law was given for a period, but only Jesus' work on the cross brought people to perfection. One died once, and for all, so now all could live for one!

Continue reading John 19:38-42.

Joseph of Arimathea, who is identified as a disciple of Jesus, asks Pilate to bury Jesus' body. The Gospel writer Matthew says Joseph was a rich man, Mark calls him "a respected member of the council," and Luke says that he "had not consented to their decision and action." It looks as if he had faith in Jesus and went against the crowd and his fellow members of the Sanhedrin. He, along with his friend Nicodemus, whom we met earlier, properly prepared Jesus for burial and laid His lifeless body in a tomb.

Reflection

1. Is sin a big deal to you? It is what sent Jesus to the cross, and it should bother us when sin is present in our lives or our culture.

2. In the cross, people either see forgiveness or foolishness. What do you see, and how does it impact your life today?

3. The cross doesn't just forgive us — it frees us. If Jesus paid for your sin fully and finally on the cross, what area of your life is He inviting you to surrender, confess, or walk in new obedience today?

Prayer

If there was a day for prayers of thanksgiving, it is today. The thought of the cross can bring many emotions. But, surely, one of thanksgiving should be true for those who are blood-bought Christ followers. The cross of Christ brought us freedom. Jesus was pierced for our transgressions; the King of Kings was crushed for our iniquities. Put on His shoulders was not just a piece of split wood, but on Him was placed the judgment for rebellion that brought us peace. By the wounds of your Savior, you can be healed. Tell Jesus what you need to say to Him in response to this.

Day 30

Sunday's Coming

John 20:1-31

Begin by reading John 20:1-10.

The silence of Saturday was surely significant. To many, Jesus was just another man sentenced and killed on a Roman cross outside the city, along with other criminals. But to others, their friend and Lord had been taken from them, beaten, and died a humiliating death He did not deserve. The fear of Friday shifted to the silence and loss of Saturday.

Each day has 86,400 seconds, but that day must have seemed longer than all the others. Where do the disciples go from here? Do they just return to their old lives like none of this happened? Do they flee to another land where maybe no one recognizes them? What do they do now that the one whom they faithfully followed is dead? Like the silence they experienced on Saturday, it is a good reminder that sometimes, God is silent in our lives because He wants to make sure we don't miss what He has to say next. And what God says and does next changes everything.

Early on Sunday morning, Mary Magdalene went to the tomb where Jesus had been laid, but to her surprise, the large stone covering the entrance had been rolled away. She quickly returned to Peter and John and told them what she had seen. They both ran to the tomb, and John humbly lets us know that he arrived first. They looked in and then went in, but the body of Jesus was not there. They just saw the grave linens folded and lying where Jesus' body should have been.

When I was 15 years old, I traveled to Israel and, while there, I discovered that there are two places people believe the tomb in which Jesus' body was laid is. One is within the old city walls and now houses the Church of the Holy Sepulchre. The other site is called the Garden Tomb, just outside the city walls. When I was there, I visited both of them. During these visits, I visited the Garden Tomb and discovered that it is maintained by a charitable trust based in the United Kingdom. There was a man with us sharing about the grounds. I clearly remember him saying in his British accent, "There is some debate on where Jesus' body was laid. Some say the Church of the Holy Sepulchre, and others, like me, believe here in the Garden Tomb. I know one thing, regardless of where His body was laid, you will not find Him there because He rose from the grave." Like many others who go to visit Israel, I stepped into the Garden Tomb and stood there for a few moments by myself, looking and thinking. As I turned to walk out, I saw written on the wall, "He is not here: for He is risen." This reality changes everything.

Continue reading John 20:11-29.

On that first Easter morning, there is an empty tomb and a risen Savior who has achieved victory over sin and death. As Jesus begins to reveal Himself, appearing before many as the risen Lord, we also see Him bringing victory over despair, doubt, confusion, fear, and failure. A new day, a new covenant, and a new opportunity for all people have come. One by one, the disciples of Jesus have an interaction with Him, including Thomas, who had told his friends, "Unless I see in his hands the mark of the nails, and place my finger into the mark of the nails, and place my hand into his side, I will never believe" (John 20:25).

We may not want to admit it, but we can all likely relate to Thomas on some fronts. Faith is not always easy. Like Thomas, we find it easier to believe in what we can see and touch. In many regards, the world we live in says seeing is believing. But if you are going to live a life of faith, you have to see it differently than the world does. Jesus also shows His patience and kindness to Thomas. Rather than saying, "Hey, knucklehead, why do you lack faith?" He tells him, in grace, to put his finger in His hands and feel His wounds. As He did for Thomas, Jesus can handle our questions and doubts. We simply must bring them to Him and ask Him to meet us in those moments. If you live in the reality that the "I Am" lives in you, you do not need to be afraid.

Finish reading John 20:30-31.

We are back where we began our first day together. Why did John write his Gospel? He meticulously shared seven miraculous signs performed by Jesus. He made sure that we knew the seven "I Am" statements that Jesus shared with His audiences. He gave us a seat in the upper room as Jesus shared His farewell discourse with His followers, and he takes us to Jerusalem for the conviction, crucifixion, and then resurrection of Jesus Christ. These are all written by John so that you may believe that Jesus is the Christ, the Son of God, and that by believing, you may have life in His name.

Reflection

1. If you believe that the tomb is empty, does your life reflect that belief?

2. "When a train goes through a tunnel, and it gets dark, you don't throw away the ticket and jump off. You sit still and trust the engineer." I once read this quote, associated with Corrie Ten Boom, who hid Jewish people from the Nazis during the Holocaust. As you read that quote, what are your thoughts related to trusting God even in tough circumstances?

3. How is your faith like Thomas's? Do you think God can handle your questions, or are you afraid to bring them to Him honestly?

Prayer

Tell Jesus that you believe that He possesses absolute authority over all things in the world and pray that you will give Him your absolute allegiance. Jesus deserves it, and we should desire to give it to Him every day of our lives. Take time declaring that to Jesus. Ask Him to continue to give you courage through diligent practice of your faith. Again, the bigger your view of God gets, the more you want to trust Him. The smaller He gets, the more you will want to control things.

Day 31 The Beginning

John 21:1-25

Begin by reading John 21:1-14.

We don't know if the guys were hungry, needed money, or just needed to do something to get their heads right. But upon their return to their home region, the seven disciples who had been together returned to the familiarity of fishing. I wonder if it was a quiet night of fishing, each thinking to himself, or if it was a reflective time, with various conversations about all that had happened. After all the disciples had experienced, surely there were many things on their minds.

After fishing through the night, the friends see the resurrected Jesus. He gives them a command, reminiscent of when He first called some of them early in His ministry. Their fishing outing had been a failure, but when He tells them to cast their nets on the other side of the boat, they recognize Him. Peter, full of emotion, leaps from the boat to get to Jesus. They all get to the shore, and Jesus already has a fire going with fish on it. I love that Jesus did not need their fish, but He invited them to contribute some of the 153 fish they had just caught to the breakfast.

Continue reading John 21:15-23.

In the intimacy of this breakfast moment, Jesus asks Peter three questions, a restorative moment following his three denials just days before. We don't fully know why Jesus kept asking Peter, but in this moment, Peter must have felt the forgiveness and love Jesus had for him. This was a moment that surely marked Peter and fueled the passion that burned in him for the rest of his life.

Early in the three Synoptic Gospels, there is a record of Jesus asking the disciples about what the crowds were saying about Him. This line of questions then gets personal, with Jesus asking them, "Who do *you* say that I am?" Peter answered, "You are the Christ, the Son of the living God." That confession remained central in the life and death of Peter.

Peter would go on to be the leader of the early church and boldly share the gospel, finally making his way to Rome. There, he was eventually crucified for his faith by the harsh Roman Emperor Nero, who later blamed Christians for a fire in Rome. Peter did not feel worthy to die in the same manner as Christ and asked to be crucified upside-down, in what is now Peter's Square in Vatican City.

According to Christian history and church records:

- Peter's brother, Andrew, took the gospel to Eastern Europe, Russia, and the churches in Asia Minor in modern-day Türkiye and Greece. He led many to Christ up until he died in Southern Greece, where he was scourged and then crucified on an X-shaped cross that is now known as St. Andrew's Cross.
- Thomas doubted no more and took the gospel to the area of Syria and as far east as India. It is said that soldiers who opposed his Christian teaching killed him with a spear.
- Philip ministered in parts of North Africa and Asia Minor, where he was put to death after leading a Roman official's wife to new life in Christ. He was crucified upside-down while he continued to preach from his cross.
- Matthew, the former tax collector and Gospel writer, ministered in Persia and Ethiopia, where it is said that he was stabbed to death at the altar by a soldier sent by the King of Ethiopia.

- Nathaniel, also called Bartholomew, spread the gospel throughout various parts of the world until he was martyred for his faith, being skinned alive and then beheaded.
- James, son of Alpheus, was arrested during King Herod Agrippa's persecution of the church, stoned, and then clubbed to death.
- Jude, also called Thaddeus, was clubbed and crucified while on a missionary trip in what many traditions place in Persia, modern-day Iran.
- Simon the Zealot preached in Egypt and Persia, where he was killed after refusing to sacrifice to a false god and then sawn in half.
- James, son of Zebedee, and brother of the author of the Gospel of John, was beheaded by a sword for his missionary work by King Herod Agrippa I, who arrested many early Christians to thwart this new movement of The Way. He was the first apostle to be martyred, and his death is recorded in the Bible (Acts 12.)
- And then there is John, the brother of James and another son of Zebedee, the disciple whom Jesus loved. He is the only one of the eleven disciples who survives all the others. He writes other letters, which later become books of the Bible, before dying in Ephesus of natural causes at an age beyond 90 years old.

Why does knowing how these men who followed Jesus died matter? Think about it. These are the same men who ran when Jesus was arrested in the garden. Most did not show their faces when Jesus hung on the cross, and they hid in an upper locked room when Jesus was placed in a borrowed grave. It is hard to think they went from being scattered and scared to being sure and willing to die for something or someone they did not believe in. No, these brothers had seen and interacted with the risen Lord. And now, they lived with their greatest asset being God living in them and the Spirit guiding them. They responded once to Jesus' call to follow Him, and again after the resurrection. "Follow me" became their life's mission, and that invitation is still open to you today.

Finish reading John 21:24-25.

Don't miss how the book of John ends, as I bring your attention to this once more, "Now there are also many other things that Jesus did. Were every one of them to be written, I suppose that the world itself could not contain the books that would be written." Think about all we have read and experienced together in our look at the Gospel of John. It is just a glimpse of all Jesus did in the flesh. Give Jesus your heart, head, and hands, and let His story be yours. Let this story we have read together drive you, and let God's Spirit guide you.

Reflection

1. Like Peter, there should be purpose in your heart and mission in your mouth. What do you think God is calling you to do this week?

2. Here is a good way to think about your life with Jesus. Draw a ccle. Step inside the circle. Ask God to start a revival in everything within the circle. It is easy to want Him to do something in other people, but maybe it needs to begin in and through you.

3. A friend of mine says, "God desires a prepared messenger more than just a prepared message." We began with John the Baptist in our time together, who was a messenger pointing to Christ. How has this time with John prepared you as a messenger, and what is your message?

4. Charles Spurgeon once said, "Every Christian is a missionary or an imposter." Which of those realities is evident in your life?

Prayer

Take a few moments and let God know He is worthy! Give God the honor that only He deserves. Tell Him how great He is and thank Him for His never-ending love. Thank God for giving us His Son and the provision and payment He made on our behalf. Ask God to help you deposit His Word in your heart and depend on His Spirit throughout your life. Offer to God a surrendered heart that is ready to proclaim the hope of the gospel to whomever you come into contact with, wherever He sends you. Thank the Lord for our time in John and what it has taught you. Ask God for wisdom on what to study next.

Do You Know Jesus?

Maybe you've turned to this page for the first time, having never entered into a saving relationship with Jesus, and are curious about what that entails. Maybe you're ready to enter into a saving relationship with Jesus for the first time. No matter where you find yourself, this page is for you. If you need to know Jesus, this page is an excellent place to start.

To enter into a saving relationship with Jesus, you first must understand who God is.

First, God is the Creator (Gen 1:1). He created everything, even you. Second, God is perfect in all His ways (Ps. 18:30). So, combined, that makes God the perfect creator of all things. He rules over everything, and His rule is 100% right.

Next, you must accept that your sin is a problem (one that you can't solve on your own).

Because God is the perfect King, when we do something that goes against His ways, it's called sin. And because God is who He is, all sin is rebellion against Him (Ps. 51:3-4). The only right penalty for our rebellion? It's death (Rom. 6:23). Both spiritual and physical. The worst part is that we're entirely unable to save ourselves.

Then, you must grasp the truth that Jesus is the only answer to your sin problem.

Jesus was God's Son, sent to earth to live a perfect life that He might serve as the once-and-for-all perfect sacrifice in our place (Matt. 1:18-21). Jesus died on the cross to satisfy God's sense of justice and to save from their sins all who will believe in Him (Jn 3:16). Only Jesus could do this.

Finally, you must believe in your heart that Jesus is who He says He is and that His death accomplished what He said it accomplished.

The only way to save ourselves from sin is to believe that Jesus is who He says He is. When we put our faith in Jesus as our Savior, we're saved from the penalty of our sin. We're saved from death. This is only possible by God's grace through faith in Jesus. We can't do anything to earn our salvation.

Here's the coolest part: When you come to salvation in Christ, your life is completely renewed, freed from the effects of sin (2 Cor. 5:17). You are a new creation!

If today is the day you choose to trust Jesus, you don't need special words or a perfect prayer. You simply need an honest heart turned toward Him. Talk to God right where you are and tell Him you believe, that you're ready to surrender your life to Christ, and that you want to walk in the new life He offers. Then tell someone. Find a church. Open the Bible. Begin building your life on the truth you've just received. Faith in Jesus is the beginning of the most extraordinary journey you'll ever take. And you will not walk it alone.

About the Author

J. Roger Davis has been creating and giving leadership to excellent, gospel-centered ministry events and mission experiences since 1993. Throughout his career, he has focused on creating moments that matter and providing resources that enable people to have a real interaction with God, shaping how they view God, themselves, the world, and their opportunity to be a person of impact. He is energized by the opportunity to help people get the gospel and give it away.

Roger currently serves as the President of *YM360*, gives executive leadership to *Servant Life Missions,* and is also a partner with *Fund The Nations*. His life and leadership roles have led to extensive travel domestically and to 50+ countries around the globe. He has also authored *John: The Way, The Truth, The Life* a devotion for teenagers as well as numerous books in the *Games For Youth Ministry* line, both published by YM360. Roger supports the Tennessee Vols and is a big Dallas Cowboys, Los Angeles Dodgers, and San Antonio Spurs fan (where he used to be a ball boy).

He and his wife, Becca, live in Birmingham, AL, with their four kids, Sterling, Landry, Kinsley, Murray, and their labs, General and Manning. Their family is active members at *The Church at Brook Hills,* where Roger continues to lead students and adults every week.